IPHIGENIA
IN TAURIS

Also available from Waveland Press

Johann Wolfgang von Goethe
Götz von Berlichingen: A Play
Translation and Introduction by Charles E. Passage

Gerhart Hauptmann
Three Plays: The Weavers, Hannele, The Beaver Coat
Translation by Horst Frenz and Miles Waggoner
Introduction by Horst Frenz

Novalis
Henry von Ofterdingen: A Novel
Translation and Introduction by Palmer Hilty

JOHANN WOLFGANG von GOETHE

IPHIGENIA IN TAURIS

A Play in Five Acts

Translated by
CHARLES E. PASSAGE

WAVELAND PRESS, INC.
Prospect Heights, Illinois

For information about this book, write or call:

Waveland Press, Inc.
P.O. Box 400
Prospect Heights, Illinois 60070
(847) 634-0081

INTRODUCTION

It is an arresting fact that the twentieth century is in possession of far more information about Homeric Greece and its antecedent eras than has been known for over two millennia, far more, in fact, than the Greeks of the classical fifth century B.C. themselves knew. Archeology, above all, has yielded this information, but important interpretations of the data have been made possible by independent discoveries in the studies of comparative religion, comparative folklore, and comparative linguistics. None of this new information, however, will shed light on Goethe's *Iphigenia in Tauris,* for this play is a work within the Hellenism of Renaissance and neo-classical traditions, which knew nothing of Heinrich Schliemann or Sir Arthur Evans, nothing of Jane Harrison or Sir James Frazer.

This is not to say that Goethe's post-Renaissance and neo-classical Hellenism was benighted. Rather, it was a nobly humanistic ideal, shared, in different ways as their temperaments differed, by Milton and Racine, by Gluck and Winckelmann. Greek and Latin scholarship provided its substance, the dignity of mankind was the fixed conceptual star of its course, and its creative method was the free and erudite manipulation of old materials within a twenty-five-hundred-year-old tradition. A fusion, in varying degree, of pagan and Christian elements was characteristic of it, as was a certain lack of historicity that tended to see Greece and Rome as a unity. To those who held this view the baffling mystery of the Homeric poems seemed to occur in a luminous glory before the beginning of history, while the First Olympiad of 776 B.C., itself a half-legendary event, was felt to initiate "classical civilization," which then spanned more than a thousand years down to a close amid the dismal triumph of the barbarians in 476 A.D. Thus in Goethe's "Mycenaean" age, for example, Roman Diana, not Greek Artemis, is in all appropriateness the name of the heroine's protecting goddess.

By definition, this post-Renaissance and neo-classical Hellenism was scholarly and aristocratic. The art works it inspired from the sixteenth to well into the nineteenth centuries addressed themselves to a cultural elite, among whom the artists might count on the acceptance of such ideas as international unity of culture founded on the classics, thoughtful conservatism, self-evident moral responsibility of good men everywhere, and pride in their participation, through education, in a noble tradition. That cultural elite tended also to agree that art in general and the drama in particular should be didactic as well as pleasing, that it most properly dealt with ethical considerations, and that it should be an educational experience on the loftiest plane for mature adults.

Western European civilization has, for better or worse, turned a significant corner since the days when those views were held. There is, accordingly, a certain distance between Goethe and the modern reader. But there is ample reward for those who are willing to traverse that distance in order to arrive at the fine poetic drama which Goethe completed, after ten years of intermittent labor, late in 1786.

It was from Herder in 1770 that the twenty-one-year-old Goethe first learned to study ancient Greek literature. Young Werther therefore read the *Odyssey* with high enthusiasm, and the youthful author himself left the fragment of a *Prometheus* drama, dated 1774. But the notion of a play about Iphigenia first occurred to him in 1776, according to a statement he made to his secretary Eckermann in 1831. Three years elapsed before pen was set to paper. Then, on February 14, 1779, as we learn from the author's diary, composition was begun in the garden house to the music of a quartet Goethe had installed there in order to "soothe the soul and release the spirits." The diary entry for February 24th says he "dreamed of Iphigenia last night." On March 8th a friend came upon him in the town of Buttstedt working at a table alternately on the drama and on the routine business of enlisting recruits, at times so absorbed as not to be aware of the recruits standing all around him. For March 19th the author dictated many years later this statement to Eckermann:

"Schwalbenstein near Ilmenau. *Sereno die, quieta mente,* after a deliberation of three years, I wrote the fourth act of my *Iphigenia* in one day."

On March 28th the work was completed.

This work, so slowly matured for three years in the author's mind and so swiftly executed in written form in six weeks' time, was a version in "rhythmic prose," which was yet to undergo painstaking revision. Nine days after its completion, on April 6, 1779, it was given a unique and ideal première. The scene was the ducal gardens in Weimar, beneath the open sky. Goethe himself played Orestes, while the title role was assigned to the beautiful professional actress of classical heroines, Corona Schröter. Goethe's friend Knebel took the part of King Thoas. Pylades was enacted by the physically impressive but apparently amateurish Prince Constantin, so that, for the third performance, Duke Carl August himself took over the role. The players were dressed in costumes approximating, as far as the study of Greek statuary would permit, authentic ancient costume, the first departure in Germany from the unhistorical "heroic costume" worn by tragic players on European stages since the Renaissance. A small and select audience was in attendance, and the author noted in his diary that night what a good effect the piece had, "especially on pure human beings."

In many respects the play constituted a tribute of almost unparalleled homage to a beloved, for Iphigenia represented, in transfigured form and with all but goddess nature, Charlotte von Stein, a living member of the Weimar court to whom Goethe was devoted in exalted love for more than ten years. Whether the real-life woman—with her husband and several children—merited such a portrait as the drama offers, posterity cannot judge. The homage, we may be sure, was wholly sincere on Goethe's part, even if the play's final revision in Italy in 1786 came very close chronologically with the author's ultimate break with the lady. In real life, he apparently felt, Charlotte von Stein had lifted from him the madness of his youth, even as Iphigenia lifts madness from Orestes. Even among the intimate audience of those initial performances only Frau von Stein knew fully what constituted that youthful madness and precisely of what her alleviation was constituted that had brought the distressed author to spiritual calm. The full significance of the words "brother and sister" must have been known to her alone, though we too may be aware that Goethe's sister Cornelia had died two years previously, and—what is more important—though we too are in possession of a poem which had gravely displeased Frau von Stein and in which the writer had expressed the poignant fancy that, in a prior existence, he had known her either as a sister or as a wife. Our drama embodies a profound psychological experience of its author's and fully merits the definition which Goethe himself assigned to all his works: "a fragment of a great confession."

A year after the première of the original "rhythmic prose" version Goethe was busily engaged in rewriting his play. Prose was again his medium, though this second version is usually printed in a quasi-metrical form termed "free iambics" (freie Jamben), now believed to be the arrangement given to the text by Goethe's friend Lavater and accepted by Goethe. These "free iambics" of the spring of 1780 yielded place in turn to a third version in the summer and autumn of 1781, still in prose but with numerous modifications in detail. By now, many of his friends, including Frau von Stein, were scrutinizing the text minutely and suggesting words and phrases to the author. Still unsatisfactory to *him*, the manuscript was among the papers he took with him when he abruptly left court, Duke, duties, and beloved to set out for Italy in 1786. There, a reading of the *Electra* of Sophocles left him discouraged with both the content, and still more with the prose form of his drama. Consultation by letter with Herder brought useful counsel about versification. A recent book on prosody by K. P. Moritz yielded further clarification and help, as Goethe explicitly acknowledged. Then, in Italy, the late months of 1786 saw the complete rewriting of the drama in the limpidly pure blank verse of the fourth and final version.

Blank verse was far from being unknown in the prosodic repertory of German poets, and scholars have listed almost a hundred instances of its use in eighteenth century compositions, even in a few dramas. Only Lessing, however, had hitherto used it in a dramatic work of high seriousness and merit, *Nathan the Wise* (1779). There the idiom had appeared stiff and awkward, whereas in *Iphigenia in Tauris* its full melodic possibilities were first made apparent. German critics are at one in praising the subtle flow and silvery sheen of Goethe's verse in this play, and indeed its beauty had much to do with making blank verse the normative idiom for the German drama just entering upon the era of its glory.

Completed in its final form on January 13, 1787, *Iphigenia* was first published in the four-volume set of *Goethes Schriften* that appeared that same year. The public was unimpressed and reviewers were cool. One of the latter remarked that it had "a few good passages and some short maxims that merit being learned by heart." German friends in Italy were equally cool. Goethe mentions their lack of enthusiasm for the work in the course of his *Italian Journey,* saying that they expected "something Berlichingian." We need to recall that the 1780's were witnessing the stormy triumphs of Schiller's early plays in all their tempestuous renewal of "Storm and Stress" and that 1787 was the very year of the highly successful *Don Carlos.* No public performances of *Iphigenia* were attempted until the Vienna staging of 1800—which was again received coolly. The Viennese public were still expecting "something Berlichingian." Nineteenth century revivals could not be described as frequent and more likely than not they were conceived as vehicles for one or another actress of established prestige. With thoughtful readers, on the other hand, the play has, generation after generation, won fervent admirers, some of them quite willing to second Thomas Mann's opinion that it should be ranked supreme among works of German literature.

The scenario for Goethe's *Iphigenia in Tauris* is to be found, of course, in the drama of the same name by Euripides. A brief synopsis of the ancient work of 412 B.C. will illuminate Goethe's methods and procedures.

The *Iphigenia in Tauris* of Euripides

Prologos
lines 1-122

Iphigenia, entering alone, declares her identity and relates the story of her apparent death at Aulis, her rescue by the goddess, and her service here in Tauris, where she merely consecrates victims to death by touching their hair, leaving their execution to others. She has had a dream which she interprets as signifying the death of her brother Orestes at home in Argos. She enters the temple to prepare a sacrifice for him.

Orestes and Pylades enter stealthily. Pylades searches the temple area while Orestes tells how he and his friend have come at Apollo's bidding to carry off the *statue* of Artemis, in return for which exploit Apollo will absolve him of the curse that is upon him for the murder of his mother. The two young men retire to await nightfall and a safer moment to seize the statue. (The ambiguity of Apollo's oracle in regard to the word "sister" in lines 2113-2117 of the play seems to have been Goethe's own invention.)

Parodos (Kommos)
lines 123-235

Enter the Chorus of captive Greek women assigned by King Thoas to Iphigenia's service. They sing a hymn in praise of Artemis, then inquire the reason for their being summoned here.

Iphigenia, coming from the temple, explains the sacrifice in honor of her dead brother. In duet, she and the Chorus make the funeral libation.

First Episode
lines 236-391

A Herdsman messenger reports to Iphigenia that he and his fellow herdsmen have seized two Greeks down at the shore after a strange scene in which one of them furiously attacked their herds with his sword under the impression that he was fighting off pursuing Furies. Iphigenia agrees to perform her deathly rite, then, after the herdsman has left, laments the cruel service to which she is dedicated.

**First Stasimon
lines 392-466**

A song of the sea, its beauties and dangers. As the Chorus women wonder who the captives may be, Orestes and Pylades are brought in under guard.

**Second Episode
lines 467-1088**

Iphigenia orders the captives to be unchained in keeping with the rules of this sanctuary. She questions Orestes, who refuses to give his name but who does relate the fall of Troy and the death of Agamemnon. Iphigenia tells him she may spare him if he will take a message back to Mycenae for her; Pylades, however, must die. Orestes refuses, but offers to die himself if Pylades may bear the message. Iphigenia agrees to this plan and goes into the temple to prepare the letter.

The Chorus commiserate with the captives. Pylades promises to marry Orestes' sister once he reaches Mycenae, to build a tomb for Orestes, and to remember him always.

Iphigenia brings the letter and binds Pylades by oath to deliver it—to Orestes, son of Agamemnon. She tells, as part of the message, how Artemis delivered her from death at Aulis and brought her here to Tauris. Orestes declares his identity and proves it with childhood reminiscences. Brother and sister recognize each other in a fine lyrical duet. Orestes ex-

plains his own journey to Tauris and
Apollo's command to carry off the
statue. They debate what is to be done.
Iphigenia offers to kill herself; Orestes
suggests they murder King Thoas, but
Iphigenia says she could not kill her
benefactor. Then she hits upon the
stratagem of carrying the statue down
to the sea to purify it in ocean water
from the taint of a murderer's presence.
She enlists the secrecy of the Chorus,
promising to take them all back to
Greece with her.

Second Stasimon
lines 1089-1152

The captive women, longing for birds'
wings, recall their cruel capture and express their yearning for home in Greece.
They sing of their excitement at the
prospect of rescue.

Third Episode
lines 1153-1233

King Thoas comes to learn whether the
two Greeks have been sacrificed. He is
confronted by Iphigenia bearing the
statute of Artemis on her way to the sea
for ritual cleansing. Thoas agrees to
order all inhabitants of the city to cover
their eyes while the procession passes
and to provide a guard for the priestess
and her two victims. Thoas goes into
the temple.

Third Stasimon
lines 1234-1283

A hymn of praise to Artemis and Apollo,
the divine sister and brother pair, in
which is related how Apollo while still
a child went to Delphi, slew the dragon
there, and made himself the god of
dreams and prophecies.

Exodos
lines 1284-1499

A messenger in frantic haste summons
Thoas from the temple to tell him how
Iphigenia's guards had waited with cov-
ered eyes by the seashore until they
feared some trick, then uncovered their

eyes just in time to see priestess and captives putting out to sea in a ship. A battle ensued, in which the Greeks were victorious. But then a sudden storm arose, driving the boat back toward shore. A second battle is now in progress and reenforcements are needed to capture the ship.

Thoas is vowing vengeance when suddenly Athena is seen in glory hovering in the air above him.

Athena bids Thoas resign himself to the will of the gods. Orestes has done Apollo's command, and she, Athena, wishes to have the statue of Artemis in her own land (Athens). From afar she instructs Orestes and Iphigenia as to what actions they must perform in Greece. Thoas acknowledges Athena's power and orders the Chorus women to be despatched also to Greece.

As the vision of Athena fades, the Chorus women sing their gratitude to her.

*　*　*

Patently, Euripides' *Iphigenia in Tauris* is not a tragedy in Aristotle's sense. In fact, it is not a tragedy at all, but a romance of adventure, and as such shows the genius of Euripides in search of a new type of drama between the extremes of tragedy and comedy. For such experimentation critics trained in the classical discipline sometimes reproach him, while German critics, with Goethe's play in mind, sometimes reproach him for glorifying the ethics of expediency. Escaped prisoners of war might disagree with the latter judgment. Be that as it may, Euripides' Iphigenia puts Greece and family and fellow countrymen above mere barbarians and is willing to lay down her life, if necessary, for the former; Thoas is gullible; Orestes and Pylades do their utmost for friendship's sake; and the gods are benign even if they work in mysterious ways. We might expect Artemis to appear for the final setting to rights, especially since the scene is her own temple grove, but Athenian patriotism brings Athena in her stead, and the commands of this latter goddess include some injunctions concerning a certain shrine in Athens which the audience might well see on their way home from the play. If this old Greek work is not the world's greatest drama, it is still poetically and dramatically moving. By no means is it dusty with centuries.

Patently, Goethe's *Iphigenia in Tauris* is neither a modernization nor a correction of its Greek predecessor, but a free reworking of the scenario for wholly new and independent purposes. The reworking was undertaken in the conviction that literature properly consisted of the retelling of age-old stories in new ways and in new combinations within the limits of classical tradition. Thus in so far as he wished to include antecedent action and details about his heroine's ancestry Goethe felt free to draw upon miscellaneous ancient sources and to interpret the data he found there in ways that seemed best to him. Several details he borrowed from the dull little school handbook of mythology known as the *Fabulae* of Caius Ilius Hyginus, a freedman of the Roman emperor Augustus. Beyond question he was aware that antiquity knew two conflicting traditions concerning Iphigenia, one to the effect that she had died on the sacrificial altar at Aulis that the Greek fleet might have sailing winds to Troy, the other to the effect that she had not died there but had been rescued by the goddess Artemis, who left a fawn to be slain in her stead. To the latter version he was committed as the datum of Euripides' play and his own, but for clarity's sake it is worth reviewing the divergent traditions briefly here.

Three daughters of Agamemnon are alluded to in the *Iliad*, but Iphigenia is not mentioned; Orestes is said to have killed Ægisthus, his mother's paramour, but the manner of his mother's death is not made clear; there is no talk of his blood guilt. The *Odyssey* adds supplementary details without essentially altering the story. Orestes, for instance, returns to Mycenae from Athens in the eighth year of the joint rule of Clytemnestra and Ægisthus since the slaying of Agamemnon, but still it is only Ægisthus whom he kills; the queen's own death is obscure as before. As for Iphigenia, we suspect that she had an origin quite apart from the family of Agamemnon, for the poet Hesiod identified her with the wild land of Thrace, to the north of Greece, where he said she was known as the barbarian goddess Hecate. Stasinus, a poet of the seventh century B.C. first (in preserved literature) told the story of her apparent sacrifice at Aulis and subsequent removal to barbarian Tauris, the modern peninsula of the Russian Crimea which juts down from the northern shore of the Black Sea. On the other hand, the lyric poets Stesichorus (630-550 B.C.) and Pindar (522-443 B.C.) declare that she indeed perished on the altar at Aulis. Æschylus in *Agamemnon* and Sophocles in *Electra* agree on her death; Euripides in his drama preferred the rescue-version, as did the Latin mythologists Hyginus and Ovid. The twin motifs of Orestes' deed of matricide and his subsequent hounding by the Furies is first attested by the post-Hesiodic poets mentioned before, and the mighty story of his guilt and atonement was of course given its supreme expression in the Æschylean trilogy of dramas, the *Oresteia*.

Absent from Goethe's drama are chorus and self-manifesting goddess, not because modern audiences could not be reconciled to either ancient usage, but because Goethe wished to present human problems within a wholly human frame of reference. Moreover, his long years of close acquaintance with Racinian drama had inevitably impressed Racinian qualities upon his poetic conception. Yet he did not use the stock figures of the confidant and confidante with which French classical tradition had replaced the ancient chorus. From Racine's *Iphigénie en Aulide* he took the convenient name Arcas (Arkas) for the character who performs the functions of Euripides' unnamed Herdsman and Messenger characters, and from a general acquaintance with Racine's works came most likely the motif of *la belle passion* —which Goethe holds in a subordinate place—felt by King Thoas for his fair prisoner.[1]

---

[1] It is hardly necessary to recur to a series of Iphigenia-plays of the late seventeenth and early eighteenth centuries on the assumption that Goethe exhaustively reviewed all treatments of the subject before starting his own

The fair prisoner herself, who could so easily have been assigned a conventionally theatrical and pathetic role, becomes in Goethe's play a profound character subjected to an intimately subtle analysis. A mere girl at the moment of her summons to the sacrificial altar at Aulis, she has spent these ten years and more since her miraculous rescue by Diana among an alien and barbarous people from whom she has held severely aloof despite all the reverence with which they have treated her. She is now a mature human being. Grief has quickened her compassion, solitude has deepened her understanding. She has immense capacities for devotion and love. Yet she is utterly alone, with affections uncommitted, with thoughts fixed frustratingly on remote and unattainable home. Upon the people around her she exerts, it is true, a beneficent influence, but she does so impersonally, almost without effort, and in the last analysis with a certain condescension. In Act I she is confronted with her first challenge in the all but unavoidable invitation to commit herself wholly and with dignity by becoming the wife of her middle-aged and noble-minded benefactor, King Thoas. She refuses. The refusal troubles her, and in her belated declaration of her identity we note in her the first stirrings of a sense of duty to fellow human beings, indeed the first stirrings of genuine awareness of actual human beings around her. The thought that her refusal will result in resumption of Taurian cruelties, long abrogated out of deference to her, weighs on her conscience. Hitherto she has remained neither Greek nor Taurian. Even her service to Diana has been reluctant and half-hearted. She has been alone in a twilight zone on the very periphery of human fellowship. She now senses that she must emerge from her spiritual isolation.

---

work, though some of these should be mentioned as indications of the popularity of the theme: —Racine's own posthumously published (1747) fragment of an *Iphigénie en Tauride*; La Grange-Chancel's *Oreste et Pylade, ou Iphigénie en Tauride* (1734); an adaptation of the latter by Johann Elias Schlegel: *Die Geschwister in Taurien* (1737) and *Orest und Pylades* (1739); de la Touche's *Iphigénie en Tauride* (1757), and its adaptation by Guillards as the libretto for Gluck's opera of the same name, exactly contemporary in its date of 1779 with the first version of Goethe's drama.

Suddenly, with Act II, she is confronted with a second challenge to human responsibility as she talks with a fellow countryman, Pylades, and as the story of Troy's fall reawakens all her
concern for her family in Greece. With Act III still more chal-
lenges meet her. Orestes reveals himself as her brother. Saving
this dearly beloved brother and the scion of her house is urgent
duty. Saving his and her friend Pylades is almost as urgent. Yet
to save either or both of them she must betray the loving kindness of King Thoas, of the king's and her friend Arkas, and of
the whole Taurian people. The noble task of elevating a barbarian nation to humanity will need to be abandoned, will need
to be left half-accomplished, perhaps allowed to be reversed and
undone. Not least of all, she will presently have to countenance,
in the theft of Diana's sacred image, an act of near-blasphemy to
the benevolent goddess who rescued her in the direst moment
from death itself.

At the beginning of Act IV she talks with Pylades and listens
with more than half her mind to the counsel of opportunism:
escape and rescue, she is told, override all obligations and gratitude is of secondary consideration. In the subsequent dialogue
with Arkas she practices the deception in which Pylades has in-
structed her, but she does so with such divided heart that the
deception is imperfectly performed. Once alone, she expresses in
monologue her full awareness of her grim plight. Pylades returns
to urge still more vividly the necessity of following *his* line of
argument, and when she is once again alone with her conscience, she is beset with a sudden impulse to cry imprecation
upon the gods for their cruelty and injustice in placing her in
this intolerable dilemma. The impulse is to blame the gods and to
shirk her human responsibility of right decision. The thought is
close to Aristotelian *hybris*. The impulse receives abrupt check as
there recurs to her memory an old song of the Fates which told
of the *hybris* perpetrated of old by Tantalus, the ancestor of her
family. She rehearses the ancient song with awe and, as the fourth
act closes, stands poised before the moral alternatives that confront her.

At the opening of Act V Iphigenia sees all the courses of action clearly defined; she knows that a decision must be made and she knows that any choice she makes must be squared with her own conscience. Only total honesty will ultimately satisfy. She declares for Truth in the presence of all parties at the risk of her own life and of the lives of beloved friends. King Thoas, who has these ten years and more been tempered in his barbarism by the example of humanity, wavers between the exercise of his harsh prerogatives and the appeal to his justice. A natural suspicion of being duped lingers in his mind until Orestes sees that the "sister" whom Apollo charged him to remove from Tauris is his own human sister, Iphigenia, and not the sacred statue of Apollo's sister, Diana. Then only the bitterness of disappointment is left in King Thoas' heart, and with exasperation he bids his captives all go. But Iphigenia will not leave him angry, bitter, and disappointed. Her final plea rises higher than objective justice to sue for understanding and human loving-kindness. The plea reaches to the core of the King's heart. With serene resignation and controlled sadness he accedes to the inevitably right by his kindly, last "Farewell!"

The human heart, so often invoked in this drama, is not the seat of passions that issue forth to storm the citadel of hateful Reason, but rather the mid-region in which Reason and intuitive Love join in indissoluble union to guarantee the highest type of humanity. Characteristically for Goethe, this exquisite fusion is realized in a woman, with males left merely to approximate this ultimate excellence. Nevertheless all the males in *Iphigenia in Tauris* advance upward on the scale of humanity under the magic persuasion of the heroine's example. Good actions influence all human beings. The problem is to initiate the good action. Inevitably the noble creed voiced in this poetic drama must be set beside the closely parallel creeds in closely contemporary works, *Nathan the Wise* and *The Magic Flute*. Both Lessing and Mozart represent males as having superior capacity for uniting Reason and Heart for guidance of noble conduct. Yet the three works complement each other admirably, and in the juxtaposing of Nathan, Sarastro, and Iphigenia one arrives at one of the loftiest ideals of humanity that humanity has ever conceived.

THE HOUSE OF TANTALUS

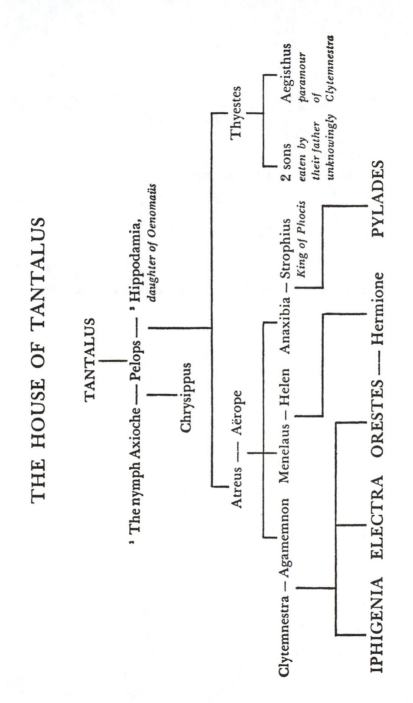

TANTALUS

¹ The nymph Axioche — Pelops — ² Hippodamia, *daughter of Oenomaüs*

Chrysippus

Thyestes

2 sons
*eaten by
their father
unknowingly*

Aegisthus
*paramour
of
Clytemnestra*

Atreus — Aërope

Menelaus — Helen   Anaxibia — Strophius
King of Phocis

Clytemnestra — Agamemnon

Hermione   PYLADES

IPHIGENIA   ELECTRA   ORESTES — Hermione

CHARACTERS

IPHIGENIA
THOAS, King of the Taurians
ORESTES
PYLADES
ARKAS

The scene is a grove in front of the temple of Diana.

ACT I

IPHIGENIA: Out here into your shadows, stirring treetops
Of this thick-branching, ancient, sacred grove,
As in the goddess' own hushed sanctuary,
I even now step with a shuddering awe
As though my foot fell here for the first time,
And here my spirit cannot feel at home.
These many years I have been hidden here
By a high will unto which I submit,
Yet I am ever, as at first, a stranger.
For, ah! the sea divides me from my loved ones,   10
And by the shore I stand whole long days through
With my soul searching for the Grecian land,
And only muted tones amid its roaring
Does the wave bring in answer to my sighs.
Alas for one who far from parents, brothers,
And sisters leads a lonely life! From his
Lips grief will eat the closest joys away,
His thoughts forever go a-swarming off
Toward the halls of his father, where the sun
Revealed the heavens first to him and where   20
At play those born with him bound firm and firmer
The tender bonds that knit them to each other.
I do not argue with the gods; and yet
The lot of women is a piteous thing.
At home or in the wars a man commands,
And in far lands he still can make his way.
Possession gives him pleasure, victory crowns him.
A death with honor will be his at last.
How close restricted is a woman's joy!

21

Even obeying a harsh husband is   30
A duty and a comfort; but how wretched
If hostile fate drives her to alien lands!
Thus Thoas holds me here, a noble man,
In solemn, sacred bonds of slavery.
O with what shame it is that I acknowledge
I serve thee, Goddess, with a mute reluctance,
Who rescued me! My life was to have been
Consigned to thee in voluntary service.
I have, moreover, trusted in thee ever
And now trust in thee still, Diana, who   40
Didst take me in thy holy, gentle arm,
The outcast daughter of the mightiest king.
Yes, Zeus's daughter, if thou didst conduct
That lofty man whom thou didst plunge in anguish
Demanding his own daughter so that he,
The godlike Agamemnon, brought his dearest
Possession to thy altar, if thou didst
Guide him with fame from Troy's walls overthrown
Back to his fatherland, preserving for him
His spouse and treasures, Electra and his son:—   50
Then bring me too back to my own at last
And save me, whom thou once didst save from death,
From this life here as well, a second death!

[Enter Arkas.]

ARKAS: The king has sent me here with offer of
His salutation to Diana's priestess.
This is the day when Tauris thanks its goddess
For freshly gained and wondrous victories.
I hasten in advance of king and army
To say that he and they are now approaching.

IPHIGENIA: We are prepared to meet them worthily.   60
Our goddess too with favoring glance expects
The welcome sacrifice from Thoas' hand.

ARKAS: Would that I also found the worthy and
Most reverend priestess' glance as well, your glance,

O holy virgin, brighter and more radiant,
A good sign to us all. But grief still shrouds
Your inmost being up mysteriously.
In vain these many years we have been waiting
For one confiding word out of your heart.
As long as I have known you in this place,   70
This is the glance at which I always shudder,
And still your soul remains close riveted
As though with bonds of iron in your bosom.
IPHIGENIA: As best becomes an exile and an orphan.
ARKAS: Do you feel you are exiled here and orphaned?
IPHIGENIA: Can foreign lands become our native land?
ARKAS: Your native land is now quite foreign to you.
IPHIGENIA: And that is why my heart is never healed.
In earliest youth, when yet my soul was scarcely
Attached to father, mother, brother, sisters,—   80
Those newer scions, lovely and together,
Were seeking to grow skywards from the base
Of ancient trunks,—an alien curse descended
Unfortunately upon me, severing me
From those I loved and rending that fair bond
In twain with iron fist. Best joy of youth
Was therewith lost and all the thriving growth
Of early years. Even in rescue, I
Was but a shadow of myself, and joy
Of life will not bloom fresh in me again.   90
ARKAS: If you term yourself so ill-fortuned there,
Then I may also say you are ungrateful.
IPHIGENIA: My thanks were always yours.
ARKAS: But not true thanks,
For sake of which a kindly deed is done,
And not the cheerful glance that shows a host
A life contented and a willing heart.
These many years ago when a profoundly
Mysterious fate brought you here to this temple,
King Thoas came with favor and respect

To greet you as one whom the gods had sent 100
And these shores were then kind and friendly to you
Which formerly held terrors for all strangers
Because no one set foot within our kingdom,
Till you, who did not perish by old custom
A bloody victim on Diana's stairs.
IPHIGENIA: Life is not merely freedom to draw breath.
What kind of life is this which, like a shadow
By its own grave, I can but pine away
Here in this holy place? Am I to call it
A life of cheerful self-awareness when 110
Each day, once it is dreamed away in vain,
Prepares us for those dreary days spent by
The mournful throng of the departed dead
On Lethe's shore in self-forgetfulness?
A useless life is early death; this fate
Of women is, above all others, mine.
ARKAS: This noble pride in self-dissatisfaction
I can forgive, much as I pity you;
It robs you of the joy of life. You have
Accomplished nothing here since your arrival? 120
Who was it lightened the king's sombre mind?
And who from year to year has kept suspended
By soft persuasion that old cruel custom
Whereby all strangers lost their lives in blood
Upon Diana's altar and so often
Delivered captives from their certain death
To be returned to their own native lands?
Has not Diana, far from being angered
By lack of those old bloody sacrifices,
In generous measure heard your gentle prayer? 130
On joyous wings does Victory not attend
Upon the army? indeed, outfly its coming?
And do we not all feel a better lot
Now that the king, who so long led us wisely
And bravely, also finds a pleasure in

The mildness of your presence and has lightened
Our silent duty of obedience?
You term it to no purpose that a balm
Is shed on thousands from your very being?
That for a people, to whom a god brought you,   140
You are the fount of fresh good fortune and
On this inhospitable shore of death
You give the stranger rescue and return?
IPHIGENIA: This little soon fades from the view directed
Forward toward how much still is left to do.
ARKAS: You praise one who says what he does is naught?
IPHIGENIA: It is blameworthy to weigh out one's actions.
ARKAS: I too blame one too proud to grant true worth,
As much as one who idly vaunts false value.
Believe me and give ear to a man's word   150
Who is sincere in his devotion to you:
When the king speaks with you today, then make
What he desires to say more easy for him.
IPHIGENIA: Your every kindly word alarms me more.
I have eluded his proposal often.
ARKAS: Think what you do and what can profit you.
Since his son's death the king confides in few
Of his own people any more, and in
Those few no longer as he used to do.
He looks with envy on all sons of nobles   160
As his successor; and a lonely, helpless
Old age he stands in dread of, possibly
Bold insurrection and an early death.
Speech is not held in high esteem by Scythians,
By the king least of all. He, who is only
Accustomed to give orders and to act,
Has no skill in directing a discussion
With subtlety and slowly toward his purpose.
Do not then make it difficult for him
By a reserved denial or a willful   170
Misunderstanding. Go half way to meet him.

IPHIGENIA: Am I to speed the thing that threatens me?
ARKAS: Do you refer to his suit as a threat?
IPHIGENIA: It terrifies me more than all the others.
ARKAS: At least meet his affections with your trust.
IPHIGENIA: If he first sets my soul free of its fear.
ARKAS: Why do you hide your ancestry from him?
IPHIGENIA: Because a secret well befits a priestess.
ARKAS: Nothing should be a secret from the king.
    And though he does not ask it outright, still   180
    He feels it, feels it deep in his great soul,
    That you hold carefully aloof from him.
IPHIGENIA: He feels annoyance and ill-will toward me?
ARKAS: So it would almost seem. True, he says nothing
    Of you to me; yet certain random words
    Have shown me that his soul has firmly fixed
    On the desire of marrying you. O do
    Not, do not turn him back upon himself,
    Lest ill-will should mature within his bosom
    And horrify you and too late you think   190
    Regretfully of my well-meant advice.
IPHIGENIA: What? Can the king be planning to do what
    No noble man should think of doing if
    He loves his name and reverence for the gods
    Restrains his heart? Does he intend to drag
    Me from the altar to his bed by force?
    Then I will call on all the gods, and on
    Diana most of all, the strong-willed goddess,
    Who to her priestess, virgin unto virgin,
    Will surely lend protection readily.   200
ARKAS: Be still! Impetuous new blood does not
    Incite the king to perpetrate that sort
    Of youthful rashness. But, as his mind works,
    I fear a different harsh decision from him,
    Which he will carry out implacably,
    For his stern soul is not one to be swayed.
    Trust him, therefore, I beg you, and be grateful,

If there is nothing further you can give him.
IPHIGENIA: O tell me what else may be known to you.
ARKAS: Learn that from him. I see the king approaching.   210
   You honor him, and your own heart bids you
   Be friendly and confiding as you meet.
   A kindly word from women goes a long
   Way with a noble man.
IPHIGENIA (*alone*):   I do not see
   How I can follow this good man's advice,
   Although I gladly do my duty in
   Returning kind words to the king for his
   Kind deed. I only hope that I can speak
   With truthfulness and please the mighty man.
                              [*Enter Thoas.*]
   May royal blessings be yours from the goddess!   220
   And may she grant you victory and fame
   And riches and well-being of your people
   And the fulfillment of all proper wishes!
   That, ruling providently over many,
   You also know rare fortune more than many.
THOAS: It would suffice me if my people praised me;
   Others enjoy what I accomplish more
   Than I do. The most fortunate of men,
   Be he a king or commoner, is he
   Whose welfare is assured in his own home.   230
   You shared in my profoundest sorrow when
   My son, my last one and my best, was taken
   Away from me by swords of enemies.
   As long as vengeance occupied my mind,
   I did not sense my house's emptiness;
   But now that I have come back satisfied,
   Their kingdom overthrown, my son avenged,
   Nothing is left at home to give me pleasure.
   The glad obedience which formerly
   Would flash toward me from every eye is now   240
   Dulled with displeasure and with discontent.

Each man thinks of the future, and obeys
Me, childless as I am, because he must.
Today I come into this temple where
I often came, to sue for victory
And to give thanks for victory. One wish
Of old I bear within my bosom, which
To you is neither strange nor unexpected:
I hope, both to my people's blessing and
My own, to take you home with me as bride.   250
IPHIGENIA: Too much you offer one you little know,
O king. The fugitive stands here abashed
Before you, who upon this shore asks nothing
But rest and safety, which you have bestowed.
THOAS: This keeping secret of your origin
From me and from the lowliest of mine
Would not be right or good in any nation.
This shore strikes fear in foreigners; the law
Demands it and necessity. But you
Who here enjoy a sacred privilege,   260
Who are an alien well received by us,
Passing your days at will and inclination,
From you I hoped for such trust as a host
May rightly look for in return for his.
IPHIGENIA: If I concealed my parents' names and my
Descent, O king, it was embarrassment
And not mistrust. For if, perhaps, you knew
Who stands before you and what head curse-laden
It is you feed and shelter, horror would
Seize your great heart with an unwonted shudder   270
And then, instead of offering me half of
Your throne, you would drive me before the time
Out of your kingdom, thrusting me perhaps
Before the glad return among my own
And the end of my wanderings are destined,
Into the misery that everywhere
With cold and alien hand of horror waits

For every wanderer exiled from home.
THOAS: No matter what the gods' plan for you is,
 Or what they destine for you and your house,   280
 Still, since you have lived here among us and
 Enjoyed the sacred privilege of a guest,
 I have not lacked for blessings from above.
 It would be difficult persuading me
 That in you I protect a guilty head.
IPHIGENIA: The good deed, not the guest, confers the blessings.
THOAS: Things done for wicked people bring no blessing.
 So put an end to silence and refusal;
 It is no unjust man who asks this of you.
 The goddess trusted you into my hands;   290
 To me you were as sacred as to her.
 Let her sign be in future my law also.
 If you can ever hope to go back home,
 I will pronounce you free of all demands.
 But if the way is closed to you forever,
 Or if your race is exiled or has been
 Wiped out by some immense calamity,
 By more than one law you belong to me.
 Speak freely! And you know I keep my word.
IPHIGENIA: Unwillingly the tongue is loosened from   300
 Its bonds of old in order to disclose
 At last a secret long kept silent. For,
 Once told, it leaves the deep heart's safe-kept dwelling
 Never to return, and then works harm,
 Or, as the gods may wish it, serves some end.
 Hear: I am of the race of Tantalus.
THOAS: How calmly you make that momentous statement.
 You call your ancestor one whom the world
 Knows as a man once highly honored by
 The gods? Can it be that same Tantalus   310
 Whom Jupiter once had at board and council,
 In whose age-tempered utterances fraught with
 Deep meaning gods themselves once took delight

As in the utterances of oracles?
IPHIGENIA: He is that very one. But gods should not
Associate with men as with their peers.
The race of mortals is too weak by far
Not to grow dizzy at unwonted heights.
Ignoble he was not, nor yet a traitor;
But too great for a slave, and for a fellow   320
Of the great Thunderer a mere mortal man.
Thus his crime too was human, and their judgment
Severe. The poets sing: Excess of pride
And treachery cast him from Jove's own table
In shame down into ancient Tartarus.[1]
Alas, and all his kin then bore their hatred!
THOAS: For their ancestors' guilt or for their own?
IPHIGENIA: The mighty breast and vigorous strength of Titans
Were, to be sure, the certain heritage
Both of his sons and grandsons; but the god   330
Affixed a bond of bronze around their brows.
Wisdom and patience, sense and moderation,
These he concealed from their shy, sullen eyes,
So each desire of theirs became a frenzy,
And limitless their frenzy raged abroad.
Already Pelops of the mighty will
And Tantalus' beloved son, by murder
And treachery had won the fairest wife,
Hippodamia, Oenomaüs' child.[2]
She to her spouse's joy bore him two sons,
Atreus and Thyestes. Jealously
They marked their father's love to his first son,[3]
Who had sprung from an earlier marriage bed.
United in their hatred, this pair then
Committed fratricide as their first deed.
The father thought Hippodamia was
The murderess, and fiercely he demanded
To have his son again from her, and she
Took her own life—[4]

THOAS: You stop? Continue talking.
Do not regret your confidences. Speak. 350
IPHIGENIA: Happy the man who can recall his fathers
With joy, who with their deeds and greatness can
Regale a hearer, and with quiet pleasure
Beholds himself at the close of that fair
Succession. For a house does not produce
The monster or the demigod straight off;
Only the evil or the good in series
Will bring about the horror of the world
Or the world's joy.—Upon their father's death
The city was ruled jointly by Thyestes 360
And Atreus. But that harmony could not
Endure for long. Thyestes soon dishonored
His brother's bed. In vengeance Atreus drove
Him from the kingdom. Long before and slyly,
Thyestes, plotting grievous deeds, had kidnapped
One of his brother's sons and reared him as
His own with fond cajolery. He filled
His heart with rage and vengeance and then sent
Him to the royal city so that he
Might in his fancied uncle slay his father. 370
The youth's intention was found out; the king
Had the assassin fiercely punished, thinking
It was his brother's son whom he was killing.
Too late he learned who was expiring under
The torture there before his glutted eyes;
To clear the lust for vengeance from his bosom
He silently thought up a deed unheard of.
With feigned indifference, calmness, and appeasement
He lured his brother with two sons of his
Back to the kingdom, seized and slaughtered them, 380
And set the loathsome, grisly dish before
Their father at the first of their repasts.
And when Thyestes had been sated with
His own flesh, and there fell a gloom on him,

And he inquired about his children, thinking
He heard their voices and their footfall at
The doorway, Atreus, grinning, flung
The heads and feet of the slain lads before him,—
You turn away your face, O king, in horror!
So did the sun avert his countenance   390
And turn his car from its eternal track.
Such is your priestess's ancestral line;
And many are the dire fates of these men,
And many are the deeds of minds confused,
Which Night enfolds in heavy pinions so
That we peer only into dreadful twilight.
THOAS: Leave them concealed in silence too. Enough
Of horrors! Tell me by what miracle
It was that you sprang from that savage race.
IPHIGENIA: Atreus' eldest son was Agamemnon: 400
He is my father. I can say of him,
However, that from earliest times I have
Found him to be the paragon of men.
To him I was born as first fruit of love
By Clytemnestra, and Electra next.
Serenely ruled the king, and to the house
Of Tantalus was granted rest long missed.
But still my parents' happiness lacked for
A son, and scarcely was that wish fulfilled,
So that Orestes now, the favorite,   410
Was growing up between two sisters, when
Fresh evil came upon the carefree house.
Report has reached you of the war which brought
The total might of princes from all Greece
To camp about the walls of Troy avenging
Rape of the fairest woman. Whether they
Have won the city and attained their goal
Of vengeance, I have never heard. My father
Commanded the Greek army. But at Aulis
They waited for a favoring wind in vain;   420

Diana, angered at their mighty leader,
Held back the eager men, demanding through
The lips of Calchas the king's eldest daughter.
They lured me and my mother to the camp;
They dragged me to the altar and consigned
My head unto the goddess.—She was appeased;
She did not want my blood and wrapped me in
A cloud to rescue me;[5] inside this temple
I first regained my senses out of death.
I am that very same Iphigenia,   430
Grandchild of Atreus, Agamemnon's daughter,
The goddess' own, now speaking with you here.
THOAS: I give no greater preference or trust
To you as princess than to you as stranger.
I make my first proposal once again:
Come, follow me, and share in what I own.
IPHIGENIA: How can I venture such a step, O king?
Does not the goddess who delivered me
Have sole right to my consecrated life?
She chose this place of refuge for me here   440
And she preserves me for a father, whom
She punished quite enough by the mere semblance,
Perhaps for his old age's fairest joy.
Perhaps my glad return is close at hand;
And I, in disregard of her plan, should
Have entered into bonds against her will?
Were I to stay, I would ask for a sign.
THOAS: The sign is that you still are tarrying here.
Do not seek out excuses of that kind.
Much talk is useless to express refusal;   450
The other party only hears the No.
IPHIGENIA: Those were not words intended to deceive.
I have shown you my heart's profoundest depths.
Does your own heart not tell you how I must
Yearn with distressful feelings for my father,
My mother, and my sister and my brother?

So that amid the ancient halls, where sadness
Still sometimes whispers my name softly, joy,
As for a new-born child, may twine the fairest
Of garlands from one pillar to another?　　　　460
O if you would but send me there in ships!
You would give me and all of us new life.
THOAS:　Go back, then! Do as your heart bids you do,
And pay no heed to the voice of good counsel
And reason. Be a woman through and through,
Yield to the impulse that without restraint
Now takes and pulls you one way or the other.
Once a desire has blazed up in their bosoms,
No sacred bond will keep them from betrayers
Who lure them from their fathers' or their husbands'　　　470
Devoted arms, however long proved loyal;
And if the swift fire in their bosoms dies,
It is in vain with faith and power that
Persuasion's golden tongue will urge them on.
IPHIGENIA:　Remember, king, your noble word! Is this
The way that you return my confidence?
You did seem ready to hear anything.
THOAS:　I was not ready for the unexpected;
But I ought to have thought of that: was I
Not dealing with a woman, after all?　　　　480
IPHIGENIA:　Do not find fault, O king, with our poor sex.
Not glorious like yours, but still not wholly
Ignoble are the weapons of a woman.
I am superior to you, believe me,
In seeing more than you, your happiness.
You, unfamiliar with yourself or me,
Think closer ties will bring us happiness.
In all good courage, as in all good will,
You urge me to submit to your decision.
And I here thank the gods for giving me　　　　490
The firmness not to enter into this
Alliance of which they have not approved.

THOAS: No god speaks; it is your own heart that speaks.
IPHIGENIA: Through our hearts only do they speak to us.
THOAS: Do I not have the right to hear them too?
IPHIGENIA: The storm of passion drowns out their soft voices.
THOAS: The priestess, I suppose, hears them alone?
IPHIGENIA: The king should note them more than anyone.
THOAS: Your sacred office and ancestral right
   To Jove's own table bring you closer to   500
   The gods than me, the earth-born savage.
IPHIGENIA: Thus
   I pay for confidence you forced me to.
THOAS: I am but human, and we had best stop.
   But let my word still hold. Be priestess of
   The goddess, as she has selected you;
   Diana must forgive me though, for having
   Quite wrongly up to now and with bad conscience,
   Withheld her ancient sacrifices from her.
   No stranger comes with safety near our shore;
   He could in all times past be sure of death.   510
   Only, you, with a certain friendliness
   That touched me deeply sometimes as a tender
   Daughter's love and sometimes as the quiet
   Affection of a bride, had so involved me
   In magic toils that I forgot my duty.
   You had lulled all my senses into sleep,
   I did not hear the murmuring of my people;
   They now are loudly crying down upon me
   The guilt and blame for my son's early death.
   I will no longer for your sake restrain   520
   The mob that clamors for a sacrifice.
IPHIGENIA: I never asked you, for my sake, to do so.
   He has misunderstood the heaven-dwellers
   Who fancies them a-thirst for blood; he merely
   Attributes his own cruel will to them.
   Did not the goddess save me from her priest?
   My service meant more to her than my death.

THOAS: It ill beseems us to interpret and
Distort the sacred usages to suit
Our minds by Reason's facile variations.   530
Do your own duty, and I will do mine.
Two strangers that we have found hidden in
The caves along our shore and who bring to
My country nothing good, are in my hands.
With them your goddess shall receive once more
Her former, rightful sacrifice so long
Withheld. I'll send them here; you know your duty.

[*Exit.*]

IPHIGENIA (*alone*) : Thou hast clouds, O rescuing goddess,
Wherein to enwrap the guiltless pursued
And to waft them out of the arms of   540
Iron destiny over the sea,
Over the widest stretches of earth,
Or wherever thou deemest fitting.
Wise art thou, and thou seest the future;
The past is for thee not past and done,
And thy gaze rests upon thine own,
Just as thy light, the life of the nights,
Rests and prevails over the earth.
O withhold then my hands from blood!
Blessing and peace it never brings;   550
And the shape of one murdered by chance
Will with terror stalk the sombre
Unwilled murderer's evil hours.
For the Immortals bear love unto
The good and far-flung races of men,
And they gladly lengthen fleeting
Life for a mortal, willingly granting
To him some small share of the cheering
View of their own everlasting sky
For a certain measure of time.   560

ACT II

Orestes. Pylades.

ORESTES: It is the path of death that we are treading;
With every step my soul becomes more silent.
When I implored Apollo to remove
The ghastly company of the avenging
Spirits[1] from my side, he seemed to promise
Aid and deliverance in the temple of
His much-loved sister who rules over Tauris,
In godlike words of hope and certainty.
And now it is fulfilled that all distress
Is to be ended wholly with my life.   570
How easy it becomes for me, whose heart
Was crushed, whose sense was numbed by a god's hand,
To bid the fair light of the sun farewell.
If an end crowned with victory in battle
Is not vouchsafed to Atreus' son and grandson,
If like my forebears, like my father, I
Must like a beast of sacrifice die bleeding,
So be it! Better here before the altar
Than off in some abandoned corner where
The nets of murderers close of kin are spread.   580
Till then leave me in peace, ye Subterraneans,
Who like loosed dogs pursue and snuff the scent
Of blood that oozes with my every footfall
To make my path a trail for you to follow!
Leave me, I will come down among you soon;
The light of day shall not see you or me.
The fair green carpet of the earth must not
Become a sporting ground for ghosts. Down there

Below I'll come to you; there all are bound
By one fate to a dull and endless night.   590
But you, my Pylades, you wholly guiltless
Companion in my guilt and ban of exile,²
How loath I am to take you to that land of grief
Before your time! The matter of your life
Or death alone still gives me hope or fear.
PYLADES: I am not ready yet, like you, Orestes,
To go down to that realm of shades. Through all
The tangled paths that seem to lead down to
Black night, I still keep thinking of how we
Can wind our way back up to life again.   600
I do not think death; I keep pondering, listening
To see whether the gods are not preparing
Some way and means of glad escape for us.
Death, whether feared or not feared, still will come,
Beyond our powers to resist it. When
The priestess lifts her hand to cut our locks
Of hair in sign of consecration, my
Sole thought will be of rescue for us both.
Raise up your soul out of this gloominess;
By doubting, you bring danger on. Apollo's   610
Pronouncement was: a sister's sanctuary
Contains your hope and comfort and return.
The words of gods are not ambiguous,
As downcast people in their gloom imagine.
ORESTES: It was already round my tender head
My mother cast the darkling veil of life,
And thus I grew to manhood, the image of
My father, and my silent glance was bitter
In its reproach to her and to her lover.
How often, when beside the fire Electra,   620
My sister, would be sitting in the hall,
I used to crowd up sorrowing against
Her lap and stare with great eyes up at her
As she shed bitter tears. Then she would tell

Me many things about our noble father;
How much I longed to see him, be with him!
Now I would wish myself to Troy, now wish
Him home. The day came—
PYLADES: O, let hellish spirits
Converse nocturnally about that hour!
May recollections of fair times give us   630
New strength for fresh careers of heroism.
The gods have need of many a good man
To do their service on this earth. And they
Have reckoned on you also; they did not
Allow you to accompany your father
When he unwillingly went down to Orcus.
ORESTES: O would that I had clasped his garment-hem
And followed him.
PYLADES: They who saved you watched out
For me as well; for what would have become
Of me, had you not lived, I can't imagine,   640
Because since childhood I have lived and only
Care to live with you and for your sake.
ORESTES: Do not remind me of those splendid days[3]
When your house gave me sanctuary and
Your noble father wisely and with kindness
Took care of the young blossom half-benumbed;
When you, an ever blithe companion, like
A light and many-colored butterfly
Around a sombre flower, every day
Would dart in new and playful life about me   650
And put your merriment into my soul,
Till I, forgetting my distress, would revel,
Swept off with you into vivacious youth.
PYLADES: My life began when I began to love you.
ORESTES: Say rather: "my distress," and you speak truly.
That is the worrisome thing about my fate,
That I, like an infected outcast, bear
Death and a secret sorrow in my bosom;

Let me but come to the most wholesome place,
And straightway all around me blooming faces   660
Take on the painful traces of slow death.
PYLADES: I would, Orestes, be the first to die
That death, if your breath ever spread contagion.
Am I not full of joy and spirit still?
And joyousness and love are wings that soar
To mighty deeds.
ORESTES: To mighty deeds? Yes, I
Recall the time when we saw them before us!
When we together often coursed the game
Through hills and valleys, hoping some day we,
In breast and hand our lofty forebears' equal,   670
Would hunt for monsters with our clubs and swords
And would pursue upon the trail of robbers;
Then in the evening we would sit beside
The broad sea gently leaning on each other
As waves came playing softly to our feet
And as the world so wide before us lay;
Then one of us would sometimes grasp his sword
And future deeds would come out thronging from
The night around us countless as the stars.
PYLADES: The work is endless that the soul burns to   680
Accomplish. We would like to do each deed
As grandly as it will grow and become
When after lapse of years through lands and races
The tongues of poets have increased and told it.
They sound so fine, the things our fathers did,
When, resting in the quiet evening shadows,
Youth drinks them in to the tones of a harp;
And what we do is, as it was for them,
Mere toil and idle botchwork.
Thus we pursue the thing that flees before us   690
And give the path no heed that we are treading
And hardly see the footprints of our forebears
And traces of their earthly life before us.

It is their shades we always hasten after,
Which godlike in some further distance crown
The peaks of mountains on a golden cloud.
I set no store by any man who thinks
About how nations might perhaps exalt him.
But give thanks to the gods, O youth, for their
Accomplishing so much through you so soon.   700
ORESTES: When they bestow a glad deed on a man
So he averts misfortune from his people,
Extends his kingdom, makes his frontiers safe,
And ancient enemies flee or are slain,
Then he has cause for thanks, because a god
Has granted him life's prime and final joy.
Me they selected as a butcher, as
My mother's murderer, though I did revere her,
And then, avenging shamefully a deed
Of shame, destroyed me with a nod. Believe me,   710
They meant to ruin Tantalus's house,
And I, the last thereof, shall not die free
Of guilt nor honorably.
PYLADES: The gods do not
Avenge the fathers' misdeeds on the son;
And each man, good or evil, carries off
His own reward with his own action. We
Are heirs to parents' blessings, not their curses.
ORESTES: Their blessing did not bring us here, I fancy.
PYLADES: And yet it was at least the high gods' will.
ORESTES: Their will it is, then, that destroys us.   720
PYLADES: Do as they bid you do, and wait. Once you
Have brought Apollo's sister to him and
Once both of them, united, dwell at Delphi,
Reverenced by a nobly thinking people,
That high pair will be graciously disposed
Toward you for that deed's sake, and they will rescue
You from the Subterraneans. None of them
Has so far dared come to this sacred grove.

ORESTES: Thus I will have at least a quiet death.
PYLADES: I think quite differently, and not without   730
   Some cleverness I have linked up things past
   With things to come and have it all worked out.
   Perhaps the great work has been ripening
   This long while in the planning of the gods.
   Diana longs to quit this harsh shore of
   Barbarians and their blood-stained human victims.
   We were appointed for that noble purpose,
   It is enjoined on us, and we have strangely
   Been brought by fate already to this portal.
ORESTES: With rare skill you entwine the gods' devices   740
   And your own wishes neatly into one.
PYLADES: What good is human shrewdness if it does
   Not harken heedfully to that high will?
   A noble man who has done many wrongs
   Is summoned by a god to some hard action
   And charged to end what seemed impossible
   To us. The hero triumphs, by atonement
   Serving the gods and this world that reveres him.
ORESTES: If I am destined to live on and act,
   Then from my laden brow let some god take   750
   Away the giddiness which on this path,
   Wet with my mother's blood, keeps dragging me
   Down toward the dead. And let him mercifully
   Dry up the spring that keeps bedashing me
   As it spurts up out of my mother's wounds.
PYLADES: Wait with more calm! You make the evil worse
   And take the Furies' office on yourself.
   Just let me do the thinking, and be quiet.
   If our joint strength is needed for some action,
   Then I will call on you, and we will both   760
   Advance with well-planned daring to achieve it.
ORESTES: I hear Ulysses speaking.
PYLADES: Do not scoff.
   Each man must choose the hero after whom

He toils to scale the pathways up Olympus.
Allow me to acknowledge that, to me,
Cunning and shrewdness do not seem disgraceful
To any man who is bent on bold deeds.
ORESTES: I like one who is brave and yet straightforward.
PYLADES: Therefore I have not asked you for advice.
    One step already has been taken. From   770
    Our guards I have cajoled much information.
    I know there is a strange and godlike woman
    Who has been holding this blood-law in check;
    A pure heart, prayer, and incense are the things
    She offers to the gods. This kindly woman
    Is much extolled; they think she is descended
    From the race of the Amazons and that
    She has fled to escape some dire misfortune.
ORESTES: It seems that her enlightened sway lost force
    In the offender's presence, whom a curse   780
    Pursues and covers like a widespread night.
    The pious bloodlust sets the ancient custom
    Free of its check in order to destroy us.
    The savage notions of the king will kill us;
    A woman can not save us if he rages.
PYLADES: Lucky for us it is a woman! Men,
    Even the best of them, become enured
    To cruelty, and in the long run make
    A law out of the thing which they abhor,
    Grow harsh from habit and unrecognizable.   790
    A woman will stand fast by one decision
    That she has made. You may more surely count
    On her in good things as in evil.—Quiet!
    She comes. Leave me alone with her. I dare
    Not name our names to her at once or trust
    Our fate to her without reserve. Go now,
    I'll seek you out before she talks to you.
                  [*Exit Orestes.*
                  Enter Iphigenia.]

IPHIGENIA: Declare, O stranger, whence you have come here.
It seems to me I should compare you rather
To a Greek than to any Scythian.[4]   800
(She removes his chains.)
The freedom I give you is ominous,
And may the gods avert what now impends!
PYLADES: O lovely voice! O welcome, welcome sound
Of one's maternal tongue in a strange country!
The blue hills of my fathers' harbor I,
A captive, see before my eyes again,
Welcome anew. And of this joy let me
Assure you: I too am indeed a Greek.
I had forgotten for a moment how
Much I have need of you, and I allowed   810
My mind to dwell on your august appearance.
O tell me, if some destiny has not
Sealed up your lips, from which one of our houses
It is you trace your godlike ancestry.
IPHIGENIA: The priestess, chosen and ensanctified
By her own goddess, now addresses you.
Let that suffice you; tell me who you are
And what disastrously prevailing fate
Has brought you to this place with your companion.
PYLADES: I can tell you quite easily what evil   820
Pursues us with its tedious company.
O if you could grant us with equal ease
The cheering glance of hope, exalted lady!
We are from Crete, and sons of King Adrastus:
I am the younger, Cephalus by name,
And he Laodamas, the eldest of
The house. Between us was a middle brother,
Harsh and wild, who in the earliest play
Of youth already spoiled our joy and concord.
We quietly obeyed our mother's word   830
As long as our sire's strength fought before Troy;
But once he had come, booty-laden, home

And soon thereafter died, we brothers were
At odds for kingdom and inheritance.
The eldest had my preference. He slew
Our brother. For that blood-guilt he is driven
With vehemence by the Fury round about.
But to this savage shore we have been sent
By Delphian Apollo with high hope.
Within his sister's temple he bade us   840
Expect to find the blessed hand of help.
As you know, we were captured and brought here
And marked for you as sacrificial victims.
IPHIGENIA: Troy fell? Dear man, assure me that it did.
PYLADES: It fell. May *you* assure us of deliverance!
And hasten the assistance that a god
Has promised us. Have pity on my brother.
O speak some words of kindness to him soon.
But spare him when you speak to him, I beg
You earnestly, for he is easily   850
Disturbed and shaken to his inmost being
By joy and sorrow and by memories.
A feverish madness sometimes comes upon him
And his free, noble mind on those occasions
Becomes the prey of the tormenting Furies.
IPHIGENIA: As great as your misfortune is, I urge you:
Forget it until you have satisfied me.
PYLADES: The lofty city, which for ten long years
Resisted the whole army of the Greeks,
Lies now in ruins, not to rise again.   860
But many graves of our best men make us
Recall the shore of the barbarians.
Achilles lies there with his handsome friend.
IPHIGENIA: So you divine forms too have turned to dust!
PYLADES: And Palamedes, Telamonian Ajax,
They never saw their fatherland again.
IPHIGENIA: He does not speak about my father, does
Not name him with the slain. He is alive, then?

And I will see him. O take hope, dear heart!
PYLADES: But blessèd are the thousands who there died   870
The bittersweet death at their foemen's hands;
For dismal horrors and a dreary end
For those returning home a hostile and
An angry god bestowed instead of triumph.
But does the voice of humankind not reach you?
To utmost distances it bears the news
Of the unheard-of things that happened then.
Can it be possible the grief that fills
Mycenae's halls with sighs reiterated
Should be a secret from you?—Clytemnestra,   880
With Ægisthus' help, ensnared her spouse
The day of his return and murdered him!—
Yes, you hold that king's house in reverence!
I see your bosom vainly fights against
This unexpected, monstrous news I tell.
Are you the daughter of a friend of theirs?
Or were you born adjacent to that city?
Do not conceal it, and bear me no grudge
For having been the first to tell this horror.
IPHIGENIA: Speak on. How was the fearful deed committed?   890
PYLADES: The day of his arrival, when the king,
Refreshed and soothed, stepped from his bath and asked
To have his garment from his spouse's hand,
The wicked woman cast around his shoulders,
Around his head, a many-folded web
That artfully entangled its broad meshes;
And as he strove in vain to disengage
Himself as from a net, Ægisthus struck him,
The traitor, and enwrapped thus in a shroud
The mighty king descended to the dead.   900
IPHIGENIA: And what reward was the accomplice's?
PYLADES: A bed and kingdom he already had.
IPHIGENIA: So wicked lust inspired the shameful deed?
PYLADES: And the profound sense of an old revenge.

IPHIGENIA: And what offense had the king given *her*?
PYLADES: By such a grievous deed that, if there were
Excuse for murder, she would be excused.
To Aulis he enticed her, and since some
Divinity denied the Greeks their sailing
By violence of winds, he brought his daughter,   910
His eldest-born, Iphigenia, up
Before Diana's altar, and she died
A victim for the welfare of the Greeks.
They say that an aversion was thereby
Stamped so deep in her heart that she acceded
To love-suit from Ægisthus and herself
Enmeshed her husband in the nets of ruin.
IPHIGENIA *(veiling her face)* :
It is enough. You will see me again.
                    [*Exit.*]
PYLADES *(alone)* : The fate of this king's house seems to have
    left her
Profoundly moved. Whoever she may be,   920
She probably herself once knew the king
And was, to our good fortune, sold here from
Some noble family. Be still, dear heart,
And let us with good cheer and prudently
Steer toward the star of hope that gleams for us.   (925)

ACT III

Iphigenia. Orestes.

IPHIGENIA: Unhappy man, I loose your fetters now
In token of a still more painful fate.
The freedom that this sanctuary grants
Is, like the bright and final glimpse of life
For one far gone in illness, a sign of death.   930
I still can not and must not tell myself
That you are lost! How could I consecrate
The two of you with murderous hand to death?
And no one whosoever dares to touch
Your heads as long as I am priestess of
Diana. But if I refuse my duty
Which the incensed king now demands of me,
He will choose one of my attendant maidens
As my successor, after which I can
Assist you only with my ardent wish.   940
O worthy countryman, the lowliest
Of knaves that touched at our ancestral hearth
Is, in a foreign land, supremely welcome.
How can I show you joy enough and blessing,
Who bring to me the images of heroes
Whom I had learned to reverence from childhood
And who refresh my inmost heart, bestowing
Upon it the touch of a fair, new hope?
ORESTES: Do you withhold your name and lineage
With prudent purpose, or may I know who   950
It is who comes like an immortal to me?
IPHIGENIA: You shall know who I am. But now tell me

What I learned only half way from your brother,
The deaths of those who, coming home from Troy,
Met with a harsh and unexpected fate
In silence at the thresholds of their dwellings.
I was brought young to this shore, it is true;
But well do I remember the shy glance
Which I once cast with wonderment and with
Timidity upon those heroes. They   960
Rode forth as though Olympus opened up
And sent the figures of illustrious ages
Of yore down to strike fear in Ilium.
And Agamemnon was most glorious
Of all! O tell me: he died, coming home,
By the craft of his wife and of Ægisthus?
ORESTES: He did.
IPHIGENIA: Alas for you, ill-starred Mycenae!
So Tantalus's grandsons have sown curse
On curse with full and frenzied hands! Like weeds
That wave their wild heads, all around them strewing   970
Seed thousandfold, they have begotten close-
Kinned murderers unto their children's children
For endless fury of retaliation!—
Disclose what in your brother's speech the darkness
Of fear so suddenly concealed from me.
How did the last son of that mighty race,
That gracious boy destined to be his father's
Avenger in times to come, how did Orestes
Escape the day of blood? Did a like fate
Enmesh him with Avernus' nets as well?[1]   980
Is he alive yet? Does Electra live?
ORESTES: They are alive.
IPHIGENIA: O lend me, golden Sun,
Your fairest rays and lay them down with thanks
Before Jove's throne! For I am poor and mute.
ORESTES: If you are linked by friendship to that house,
If you are bound to it by closer ties,

As is betrayed to me by your fair joy,
Then grip your heart and hold it fast! For sudden
Lapse back into the depths of grief must be
Unbearable for one in joy. I see   990
You only know of Agamemnon's death.
IPHIGENIA: Do I not have enough with that grim news?
ORESTES: You have heard no more than the half of horror.
IPHIGENIA: What else? Orestes and Electra live.
ORESTES: You have no fears for Clytemnestra, then?
IPHIGENIA: She can be saved by neither hope nor fear.
ORESTES: No, but her own blood did give her her death.
IPHIGENIA: Speak clearer words, leave me to guess to longer. 1000
Uncertainty is beating her dark wings
A thousandfold around my fearful head.
ORESTES: The gods, then, have selected me to be
The tidings-bearer of a deed which I
Should so much like to bury in the soundless
And hollow cave of night? Against my will
Your gracious lips compel me; they may even
Inquire for something painful and receive it.
   The day their father died, Electra hid
Her brother in a place of safety. Strophius,   1010
Their father's brother-in-law, gladly took him
And brought him up along with his own son,
Who, Pylades by name, formed fairest ties
Of friendship with the boy who thus arrived.
As they grew up, there grew up in their souls
A burning wish to avenge the king's death.
Unnoticed, garbed as foreigners, they reached
Mycenae, as if they were bringing there
The sad news of Orestes' death together
With his ashes.[2] There the queen received   1020
Them well; they gained their access to the house.
Orestes made himself known to Electra;
She fanned the fire of revenge in him
Which in his mother's sacred presence had

Died down to embers. Silently she led
Him to the place at which his father died
And where an old, faint trace of wantonly
Spilled blood still stained the frequently washed floor
With ominous and palely faded streaks.
She there described for him with tongue of fire   1030
Each circumstance of that outrageous deed,
Her own life spent in servile misery,
The haughtiness of the secure betrayers,
And all the dangers now impending for
The children of a mother turned stepmother;
She forced upon him there that ancient dagger
Which had in Tantalus's house raged grimly,
And Clytemnestra died by her son's hand.
IPHIGENIA: Immortal gods who live in blessedness
The pure day long on clouds forever new,   1040
Have you kept me apart these many years
From human beings, held me so close to
Yourselves, committed to my care the child-like
Employment of attending to the holy
Fire, and drawn my soul up like a flame
In everlasting, pious clarity
Unto your dwelling places, only so
That I might feel my house's horrors later
And more profoundly?—Tell me now of that
Unfortunate! Tell me about Orestes!—   1050
ORESTES: O if one only could tell of his death!
How foaming from the slaughtered woman's blood
His mother's ghost
Rose and cried unto Night's primeval daughters:
    "Let not the matricide get away!
    After the criminal! To you he is consecrate!"
They stopped and harkened, and their hollow gaze
Looked round about them with the eagle's craving.
They stirred amid the blackness of their caves
And out of corners came gliding their companions,   1060

Doubt and Remorse, so softly up to join them.
Before them rose a smoke of Acheron,[3]
And in its billowing cloud there spins forever
The image of the perpetrated deed
Bewilderingly around the guilty head.
And they with authorized destruction tread
The lovely ground of earth which gods have sown
And whence an ancient curse drove them long since.[4]
And their swift foot pursues the fugitive,
Allowing rest but to scare up anew.   1070
IPHIGENIA: Unhappy man, you are in a like case
  And feel what that poor fugitive endures!
ORESTES: What are you saying? Why is my case like?
IPHIGENIA: Like him, a brother's murder weighs you down;
  Your younger brother has already told me.
ORESTES: I cannot bear, great soul, that you
  Should be deceived by an untrue report.
  A stranger, wily and accustomed to
  Deceit, may for another stranger weave
  A web of lies to trip him; between *us*   1080
  Let there be truth.
  I am Orestes! and this guilty head
  Is bending toward the pit and seeking death;
  It shall be welcome in whatever form!
  Whoever you may be, I wish you rescue;
  I wish my friend the same—but not for me.
  You seem to tarry here against your will.
  Contrive your plan of flight, but leave me here.
  Let my dead body hurtle from the cliff
  And let my blood stream smoking to the sea   1090
  And pass its curse to this barbarian shore!
  May both of you go back home to fair Greece
  And there begin a kindly life anew.
                    (*He withdraws.*)
IPHIGENIA: So thou dost come, Fulfillment, fairest daughter
  Of mightiest Father, down at last to me!

How your form looms immense before me here;
My glance can scarcely reach up to your hands,
Which, filled with fruit and wreathèd garland-blessings,
Bring down to me the treasures of Olympus.
As kings are known by superfluity   1100
Of gifts—for to them that must seem but little
Which thousands find to be great wealth—so you,
Ye gods, are to be recognized by gifts
Long hoarded up and wisely held till ready.
For you alone know what can do us good,
You see the far-flung reaches of the future
When every evening's misted veil of stars
Conceals the prospect from us. Calmly you
Lend ear unto our supplications begging
So childishly for haste; but your hands never   1110
Pluck unripe the golden fruit of heaven;
And woe to him who in his obstinate
Impatience takes them and eats to his death
Of that sour food. O do not let this long
Awaited, scarcely dreamed-of happiness
Pass like the shade of a departed friend
Away from me in vain with tripled sorrow!
ORESTES (*who comes back to her*):
    If you are praying for yourself and Pylades,
    Do not name my name with your other two.
    You will not save the criminal whom you   1120
    Have joined, and you will share his curse and pain.
IPHIGENIA: My destiny is closely linked with yours.
ORESTES: By no means! Let me go to death alone
    And unaccompanied. If you hid me in
    Your very veil, guilt-laden as I am,
    You could not hide me from those sleepless ones;
    Your presence, O immortal one, can only
    Force them aside, not frighten them away.
    They dare not tread this sacred forest's floor
    With their audacious feet of crushing bronze;   1130

Yet from the distance here and there I hear
Their ghastly laughter. Wolves will wait that way
Around a tree in which a traveler
Has taken refuge. They lie in wait out there
Beyond; and if I were to leave this grove,
They would arise and shake their serpent-hair,
And stir the dust on every side, and drive
Their quarry on before them in his flight.
IPHIGENIA: Can you, Orestes, hear a friendly word?
ORESTES: No, save it up for some friend of the gods.   1140
IPHIGENIA: But they are giving you new light of hope.
ORESTES: Through smoke and vapor I see the dull shine
Of death's own river lighting me to hell.
IPHIGENIA: Have you Electra, just one sister only?
ORESTES: I knew that one; the eldest was, however,
Saved from our house's wretchedness in time
By kindly fate, though it seemed horrible
To us. O cease your questions and do not
Yourself join the Erinyes; they blow
The ashes from my soul maliciously   1150
And will not let the final embers of
My house's conflagration burn away
And die with me in silence. Must that fire,
Thus fanned deliberately and fed with sulphur
Of hell, burn my tormented soul forever?
IPHIGENIA: I bring sweet-scented incense to that flame.
O let love's pure breath, gently wafted, cool
The burning deep within your breast. Orestes,
My dear one, can you not hear what I say?
Has the attendance of the gods of terror   1160
So caused the blood to dry up in your veins?
Does some spell, turning you to stone, steal through
Your limbs as from the grisly Gorgon's head?[5]
O, if the voice of shed maternal blood
Can summon you with dull sound down to hell,
May not a stainless sister's word of blessing

Call down gods of assistance from Olympus?
ORESTES: It calls! It calls! Are you bent on my ruin?
Is there some vengeance-goddess hidden in you?
Who are you, you whose voice so hideously   1170
Turns back my inmost being on its depths?
IPHIGENIA: Your inmost being tells you who I am.
Orestes, it is I! Iphigenia!
I am alive!
ORESTES: What? You?
IPHIGENIA: My brother!
ORESTES: Leave me!
I warn you, do not touch these locks of mine!
As from Creusa's bridal raiment, fire[6]
Is struck and spread unquenchably from me.
Leave me! Like Hercules, I want to die
A death of shame, and closed within myself.
IPHIGENIA: You will not perish! O, if I could only   1180
Hear one calm word from you! Resolve my doubts
And let me also have some reassurance
Of happiness I have so long besought.
Both joy and sorrow sweep alternately
Across my soul. An awesome horror drives
Me back from the strange man, and yet my heart
Impels me mightily on toward my brother.
ORESTES: Is this Lyaeus' temple?[7] Is the priestess
Seized uncontrollably by holy frenzy?
IPHIGENIA: O hear me! Look at me! See how my heart   1190
After a long, long time is opening to
The bliss of kissing the head of the dearest
Person whom the world can hold for me,
Of clasping you within my arms, which were
Outstretched before to empty winds alone!
O let me! Let me! The eternal fountain
Does not more brightly pour down from Parnassus
From cliff to cliff into the golden valley
Than joy now flows up surging from my heart,

Surrounding me as with a blissful sea.   1200
Orestes! O my brother!
ORESTES: Lovely nymph,
I do not trust you or your flattery.
Diana asks that priestesses be stern
And will avenge the profanation of
Her holy place. Take your arm from my breast.
And if you wish to love and save some youth
And seek to offer him sweet happiness,
Then turn your kind heart to my friend, a man
More worthy. He is wandering along
That path there on the cliff; go seek him out,   1210
Direct him and spare me.
IPHIGENIA: Compose yourself,
My brother, realize whom you have found!
Rebuke your sister for pure joy of heaven,
And not for reckless, guilty passion.
O take illusion from his staring eyes,
So that this moment of our utter joy
Does not make us thrice wretched! She is here,
Your long lost sister. For the goddess swept me
Up from that altar and bore me to safety
To her own sanctuary here. You are   1220
A captive, marked for sacrificial slaughter,
And find the priestess to be your own sister.
ORESTES: Unhappy, wretched woman! May the sun
Then see the final horrors of our house!
Electra is not here? so she could be
Destroyed along with us and not prolong
Her life for still more grievous fate and pain.
Good, priestess: I will follow to the altar;
Fratricide has been a common habit
Among our ancient clan; and I thank you,   1230
Gods, for deciding my extermination
Without children. And let me warn you: do not
Be too fond of the sun or of the stars;

Come, follow me to the dark realm below!
As dragons spawned amid the sulphur-pit
Attack their fellow-spawn and eat them up,
Our frenzied family destroy each other.
Come down with me still innocent and childless!
You gaze at me with pity? Do not do so!
It was with such looks Clytemnestra tried   1240
To gain some access into her son's heart;
But his arm, upraised, struck her to the heart.
My mother fell!—Appear, indignant ghost!
Close up your circle and advance, you Furies,
Be present at this welcome spectacle,
The last and ghastliest you have prepared!
Not hatred, not revenge now whets her dagger,
My loving sister is compelled to do
This deed. Do not weep. You are not to blame.
I have loved no one since my earliest years   1250
The way that I could love you, O my sister.
Yes, wield your knife, do not hold back at all,
Slash wide this breast and open up a path
For all the rivers that seethe here within.
                    (*He collapses in exhaustion.*)
IPHIGENIA: This happiness and misery I cannot
Endure alone.—Where are you, Pylades?
Where can I come to find your help, dear man?
                    (*She goes out searching.*)
ORESTES (*rousing from his stupor and getting up*):
Another draught! Out of the waves of Lethe
Hand me the last cool goblet of refreshment.
Life's spasm will be quickly washed away   1260
And my heart cleansed; my spirit soon will flow
In quiet, yielding to oblivion's spring,
To you, ye shades, into eternal mists.
In your peace let the son of earth, much driven
About, come graciously to quench his thirst!
What whispering do I hear among the branches?

What sound comes rustling out of yonder twilight?
Already here to see the newest comer!
What is this host that splendidly rejoices
Together like a princely house assembled?   1270
They walk in peace, the old and young, and husbands
With wives; how godlike and how like each other
They seem to move, these forms. Yes, it is they,
The forebears of my house!—There with Thyestes
Walks Atreus in familiar conversation,
With the lads darting playfully around them.
Is there no enmity among you here?
Has vengeance been extinguished with the sunlight?
Then I too must be welcome, and I may
Join in the solemn pomp of your procession.   1280

Welcome, fathers! Orestes greets you,
The last man of all your race and line;
He has reaped that which you had sown:
With curses oppressed, he has descended.
But here every burden is lighter to bear:
Accept him, accept him into your midst!—
You, Atreus, I honor, and you, Thyestes;
Here we are all rid of enmity.—
Show me my father, whom I saw only
Once in my life!—Is it you, my father?   1290
And leading my mother so tenderly?
If Clytemnestra may give you her hand,
Orestes too may go up to her
And say to her: See your son!—
Both of you: see your son! Bid him welcome!
In our house during the earthly life
Greeting was murder's surest of watchwords,
Yet the olden race of Tantalus
Has its joys on the further side of the night.
"Welcome!" you cry, and receive me well.   1300
O take me to the old man, my ancestor.[8]
Where is the old one? Let me see him,

That beloved man and much revered
Who used to sit in the councils of gods.
You seem to shudder? You turn away?
What is it? The peer of gods is in pain?
Alas! The all-too-powerful ones
Have riveted horrible torments
To that hero's breast with iron chains.

(*Enter Iphigenia and Pylades.*)

Have you two also so soon come down?   1310
Hail, my sister! We still lack Electra:
May some kindly god quickly send us down
That *one* as well with gentle arrows.[9]
As for you, poor friend, I must pity you.
Come along, come along, to Pluto's throne
To greet our host as befits new guests!

IPHIGENIA: You brother-sister pair who for mankind
Bring up the fair light over the broad heavens
By day and night and who may not shine on
The dead departed, save us, brother and sister!   1320
Thou dost, Diana, love thy gracious brother
Above all else that earth and sky can offer,
And thou dost turn thy virgin countenance
Toward his eternal light with silent yearning.
O let not my sole, late-discovered brother
Rave in the darkness of insanity.
And if thy will, since thou hast hid me here,
Be now accomplished, and if thou wilt give
Thy blessèd help to me through him and also
To him through me, release him from this curse   1330
Before the precious time of rescue fades.
PYLADES: Now do you know us, and this sacred grove,
And this light which does not shine on the dead?
Do you feel your friend's and your sister's arms
As they still firmly hold you up alive?
Take stout grasp of us; we are not empty shades.

Mark now my word and listen closely! Pull
Yourself together! Every moment counts,
And our return depends on slender threads
Spun now, it seems, by a well-wishing Parca.   1340
ORESTES (to Iphigenia) :
O let me for the first time with free heart
Experience pure delight clasped in your arms!
Ye gods, who walk abroad with flaming might
And as you walk consume the heavy clouds,
Who, graciously-severe, upon the earth
Pour down the long-sought rain in raging streams
Amid the thunder's voice and roar of winds,
Yet presently resolve the shuddering dread
Of men to blessings, changing anxious awe
To joyous glances and loud gratitude   1350
When, in the raindrops on fresh-quickened leaves,
The new sun is reflected thousandfold
And Iris of the lovely hues with light
Hand parts the grey veil of the final clouds,—
O let me too, clasped in my sister's arms
And at my dear friend's heart, enjoy and keep
With total gratitude what you grant me!
    The curse is lifting; my heart tells me so.
To Tartarus pass the Eumenides,[10]
I hear their going, and they close behind them   1360
The doors of bronze with far-receding thunder.
The earth exhales refreshing fragrance and
Invites me to its plains for full pursuit
Of life's delights and high accomplishment.
PYLADES: Do not let slip the precious time we have!
And may the wind that swells our sails be first
To bring our utter joy up to Olympus.
Come! We need swift decision and resolve.   (1368)

ACT IV

IPHIGENIA: Once the immortals destine
  Manifold confusions
  For one of the dwellers of earth,
  Once they ready for him
  Utterly shattering changes
  Over from joy to sorrow
  And from sorrow to joy,
  Then, be it close by his city
  Or on a distant shore,
  They undertake to provide
  Him with a tranquil friend,
  So that in hours of need   1380
  There may be help at hand.
Shed blessings, gods, upon our Pylades
And on whatever he may undertake.
He is the arm of the young man in battle,
The old man's shining eye in the assembly,
For his soul is at peace, and it contains
The sacred, inexhaustible endowment
Of calm; for one much buffeted about
He fetches help and counsel from its depths.
He tore me from my brother, at whom I   1390
Had gazed and gazed in wonderment, unable
To realize my happiness; I would not
Release him from my arms and did not sense
The nearness of the danger that surrounds us.
They now have gone to carry out their plan
Down by the sea, where, hidden in a cove,
The ship with their companions is awaiting

61

Their signal. They gave me a shrewd reply
With which to make the king an answer if
He sends more urgent orders to perform   1400
The sacrifice. Oh, I can see quite well
That I must let myself be guided like
A child. I never learned to use deceit
Or how to trick things out of people. Woe!
O woe to lies! They do not liberate
The heart as other words true-spoken do.
They do not comfort us, they strike alarm
In one who secretly invents them, and,
Like arrows sped and by some god averted
And made to miss their mark, they backward fly   1410
To strike the archer. Worry after worry
Wavers across my heart. Perhaps the Fury
Will fiercely seize my brother once again
Upon the ground of the unhallowed shore.
Will they discover them? I think I hear
Armed men approaching!—Here!—The messenger
With rapid step is coming from the king.
My heart pounds and my soul is clouded over
As I catch sight of that man's countenance
Whom I must now address with falsity.   1420

[Enter Arkas.]

ARKAS: Make haste now, priestess, with the sacrifice.
The king is waiting and the people with him.
IPHIGENIA: I would obey your sign and do my duty,
But that an unexpected obstacle
Intrudes itself between me and compliance.
ARKAS: What is it that impedes the king's command?
IPHIGENIA: A chance event of which we are not master.
ARKAS: Declare it so I may report it to him,
Because he has resolved on both men's deaths.
IPHIGENIA: Such is not yet the gods' determination.   1430
The elder of these men is burdened with
The crime of bloodshed of one close of kin.

The Furies hound him on his trail; indeed
The evil came upon him in the inner
Temple itself, and that pure place has now
Been desecrated by his presence. I
Am hurrying with my maidens to perform
A mystic consecration at the seashore
And dip the goddess' statue in fresh waves.
Let none disturb our silent journey there.   1440
ARKAS: I shall with speed inform the king of this
New obstacle; do not begin the holy
Task until he has sent his permission.
IPHIGENIA: But that is left up wholly to the priestess.
ARKAS: So odd a circumstance the king must know of.
IPHIGENIA: His counsel, like his command, will alter nothing.
ARKAS: The powerful are often asked for form's sake.
IPHIGENIA: Do not insist on what I should refuse.
ARKAS: Do not refuse a good and proper thing.
IPHIGENIA: I will comply if you make no delay.   1450
ARKAS: With speed I shall bring this report to camp,
With speed I shall be back here with his answer.
Would that I could take him a further message
Resolving all the things that now distress us,
For you have left a true man's word unheeded.
IPHIGENIA: I have done gladly all that I could do.
ARKAS: It still is not too late to change your mind.
IPHIGENIA: That simply does not lie within my power.
ARKAS: You term impossible what costs you effort.
IPHIGENIA: Your wish misleads you to think it possible.   1460
ARKAS: Will you so calmly risk all that you have?
IPHIGENIA: I have laid it in the hands of the gods.
ARKAS: They tend toward human means to rescue humans.
IPHIGENIA: All things depend upon their slightest hint.
ARKAS: And I tell you it lies within your hands.
It is the king's own irritated feelings
Alone that bring these strangers bitter death.
The army long since weaned their minds away

From cruel sacrifice and bloodstained office.
Yes, many a man whom an adverse fate   1470
Has borne to alien shores, has learned indeed
How godlike is a friendly human face
Encountered by a hapless wanderer
Thus buffeted about on a strange border.
O do not fail us when you can so help us!
You easily can finish what was started,
For Gentleness, which comes in human form
Down from the skies, can nowhere build a kingdom
More readily than where, all dark and wild,
A new folk full of life and strength and courage,   1480
Abandoned to itself and dread misgivings,
Endures the heavy weight of human life.
IPHIGENIA: O do not agitate my soul, which you
    Can not prevail upon to do your will.
ARKAS: As long as time is left, one does not stint
    Exertion or a good word's repetition.
IPHIGENIA: You but distress yourself and cause me sorrow,
    And both in vain; therefore please leave me now.
ARKAS: It is to sorrow that I make appeal;
    Your sorrow is a friend and counsels well.   1490
IPHIGENIA: It seizes on my soul with vehemence,
    But yet without effacing my repugnance.
ARKAS: Can lofty souls feel such repugnance for
    A kindness that a noble man extends?
IPHIGENIA: Yes, when the noble man improperly
    Seeks, not my gratitude, but to possess me.
ARKAS: A person who feels no affection never
    Is at a loss for words of self-excuse.
    I shall inform the prince of what has happened.
    O if you only would rehearse within   1500
    Your soul how nobly he has treated you
    From your arrival to this present day!
                    [Exit.]
IPHIGENIA (alone): At this man's words I feel my heart reversed

At an unfitting moment suddenly
Within my bosom. I am terrified!—
For, as the tide in swift streams swelling breaks
Over the rocks that lie amid the sand
Along the shore, so was my inmost being
Submerged beneath a stream of joy. I held
What was impossible clasped in my arms.   1510
It seemed as if a cloud were softly closing
Again about me, lifting me above
The earth, and lulling me once more into
That slumber which the kindly goddess once
Disposed around my brow when her arm grasped
And rescued me.—My heart seized on
My brother with unprecedented force;
I harkened only to his friend's advice,
My soul urged forward only to save them.
And as a sailor gladly turns his back   1520
Upon the crags of a deserted island,
So Tauris lay behind me. Now the voice
Of this true man has reawakened me,
Reminding me that here too I abandon
Human beings. Doubly hateful to
Me is deception. O my soul, be still!
Do you begin to waver now and doubt?
The firm ground of your solitude you must
Abandon now! And once again embarked,
The waves will take you in their rocking, sad   1530
And fearful you will not know world or self.
                    [*Enter Pylades.*]
PYLADES: Where is she? so that in swift words I may
    Bring her the cheerful tidings of our rescue!
IPHIGENIA: You see me full of care and expectation
    Of the sure comfort that you promised me.
PYLADES: Your brother has been cured! We trod upon
    The rocky ground of the unhallowed shore
    And on the sand in cheerful conversation.

The grove remained behind us; we forgot it.
More splendidly and still more splendidly   1540
There blazed around his head with all its curls
The glorious flame of youth; his full eye shone
With hope and courage, and his free heart gave
Itself completely to the joy and pleasure
Of saving you, his rescuer, and me.

IPHIGENIA: All blessings be upon you! From your lips
    Which have pronounced such good things may there never
    Be heard the sound of sorrow or lament!

PYLADES: I bring still more, for splendidly attended
    Like princes is Good Fortune's way of coming.   1550
    We did find our companions there as well.
    Within a rocky cove they had concealed
    The ship and sat in sad expectancy.
    They caught sight of your brother and they all
    Leaped up exultant, urgently requesting
    The hour of departure to be hastened.
    Each hand is eager to lay hold of oars,
    And from the land a light breeze even spread
    Its lovely pinions, as we all observed.
    So let us hurry! Lead me to the temple   1560
    And let me get into the sanctuary
    And reverently seize on our objective!
    I will be able by myself to carry
    The goddess' statue on my well-trained shoulders;
    O how I yearn to bear that welcome burden!

        (As he is speaking these last words he goes
        toward the temple without noticing that Iphi-
        genia is not following him; finally he turns
        around.)

You stand and hesitate—you do not speak!
You seem confused! Some new calamity
Opposes our good fortune, then? Declare it!
Did you send to the king that shrewd reply

That we had previously agreed upon?   1570
IPHIGENIA: I did, dear man; and yet you will rebuke me.
The sight of you already is reproof.
The king sent me his messenger, and as
You prompted me to speak, I spoke to him.
He seemed to be amazed and urgently
Desired first to report this strange rite to
The king and to hear what his orders were;
And I am now awaiting his return.
PYLADES: Alas for us! The peril hovers now
About our heads anew! Why did you not   1580
Hedge yourself prudently with priestess' rights?
IPHIGENIA: I never have used them as a concealment.
PYLADES: You will, pure soul, destroy yourself and us
Together. O, why did I not foresee
Such a predicament and teach you also
How to elude such a demand!
IPHIGENIA: Blame me
Alone, the fault is mine, I realize.
And yet I could in no way else confront
That man who reasonably and seriously
Asked what my heart acknowledged was his right.   1590
PYLADES: The outlook grows more menacing; but all the same
Let us not falter or betray ourselves
By thoughtlessness and over-haste to action.
Wait calmly for the messenger's return,
And then stand firm, no matter what he brings:
For ordering such rites of consecration
Lies with the priestess and not with the king.
If he demands to see the foreign man
Who is so heavy burdened down with madness,
Decline to do so, as if you had both   1600
Of us well guarded in the temple. Give
Us time to flee in haste and steal the holy
Treasure from this harsh, unworthy people.
Apollo sends the best of omens, and

Before we have fulfilled his stipulation,
He has fulfilled his promise like a god.
Orestes has been cured, he is set free!—
O take us, favoring winds, with him set free,
Unto the rocky isle the god inhabits,[1]
Thence to Mycenae, so it may revive,   1610
So from the ashes of the burned-out hearth
The household gods may joyously arise
And lovely fire may shine about their dwellings.[2]
Your hand shall be the first to strew the incense
Before them out of golden vessels. You
Shall bring well-being and new life across that threshold,
Atone the curse, and deck anew your people
In splendor with the blossoms of fresh life.
IPHIGENIA: When listening to you, beloved man,
My soul, touched by the sunlight of your words,   1620
Turns up and faces toward sweet consolation
The way a flower turns up toward the sun.
How precious are a friend's words of assurance;
A solitary person pines away,
For lack of that celestial strength, in silence.
For thoughts and resolutions ripen slowly
Within the bosom, and a loving person's
Presence would develop them with ease.
PYLADES: Farewell. I go in haste to reassure
Our friends who wait in longing expectation,   1630
Then I will come back quickly and, concealed
Within that thicket, listen for your sign—
What are you pondering? A silent sadness
Wafts over your free brow all of a sudden.
IPHIGENIA: Forgive me! Like light mists across the sun,
Light care comes drifting on across my soul
With trepidation.
PYLADES: Do not be afraid!
Fear has allied itself deceitfully
With Peril, for those two are close companions.

IPHIGENIA: I term that care a noble one that warns me   1640
   Not to betray maliciously and rob
   The king who has become my second father.
PYLADES: You flee from someone who would kill your brother.
IPHIGENIA: It is the same man who has shown me kindness.
PYLADES: What Need compels is not ingratitude.
IPHIGENIA: Ingratitude it is,—by Need excused.
PYLADES: Before both gods and men, in your case, surely.
IPHIGENIA: My own heart is not satisfied, however.
PYLADES: Excess of scruple is a mask for pride.
IPHIGENIA: I do not analyse, I merely feel.   1650
PYLADES: If you feel rightly, you revere your action.
IPHIGENIA: Unstained alone the heart approves itself.
PYLADES: You have so kept yourself here in the temple;
   Life teaches us to be less strict both with
   Ourselves and others; you will learn that too.
   So wondrously is mankind constituted,
   So various are his knots and interweavings,
   That no one can stay pure and unconfused
   Within himself or with his fellow men.
   Nor are we called upon to judge ourselves.   1660
   To walk our way and keep our eyes fixed on it
   Is mankind's first and foremost obligation:
   They seldom judge aright what they have done
   And almost never prize what they are doing.
IPHIGENIA: You almost sway me to share your opinion.
PYLADES: Is swaying needed when choice is ruled out?
   To save yourself, your brother, and a friend
   There is but one way; can we help but take it?
IPHIGENIA: O let me hesitate! for you would not
   Do such wrong calmly to a man to whom   1670
   You felt yourself indebted for kind treatment.
PYLADES: If we are lost, a still more harsh reproach
   Awaits you, and it will include despair.
   You are not used to losing, obviously,
   Since, to escape a major evil, you

Won't sacrifice so much as one false word.
IPHIGENIA: If I but had a man's heart in my bosom,
　Which, when it entertains a daring notion,
　Will shut itself to every other voice!
PYLADES: It is in vain that you refuse; the iron   1680
　Hand of Necessity commands, and its
　Stern beckoning is supreme law, to which
　The gods themselves must bow. In silence rules
　Eternal Destiny's unhearing sister.
　What she enjoins upon you, bear, and do
　As she commands. The rest you know. I shall
　Be back here quickly to receive the fair
　Seal of deliverance from your sacred hand.
　　　　　　　　　　[*Exit.*]
IPHIGENIA (*alone*): I must comply, for I see my own people
　In urgent danger. But alas for me!   1690
　My own fate makes me ever more distressed.
　O, may I not still salvage that soft hope
　That I had cherished in my solitude?
　Is this curse to endure forever? Is
　This house then never to arise again
　With a fresh blessing?—All things else decline!
　The best of happiness, life's fairest strength
　Will slacken finally: why not this curse?
　Have I then hoped in vain, preserved out here
　And cut off from my house's destiny,   1700
　To expiate with pure hand and pure heart
　Some future day that dwelling so defiled!
　Within my arms my brother scarcely has
　Been cured from dire ill by a sudden marvel,
　A ship long prayed for scarcely comes in sight
　To take me to a harbor of my forebears,
　When deaf Necessity with hand of brass
　Imposes sin twofold upon me: stealing
　The sacred statue much revered and trusted
　Into my keeping, and deceiving someone   1710

To whom I owe my life and destiny.
O let not an aversion spring up in
My bosom finally! And may the hatred
That those primeval gods, the Titans, feel
Toward you, Olympians, not rend my tender
Bosom also with its vulture claws![3]
Save me and save your image in my soul!
   My ears are humming with an ancient song—
I had forgotten it, and gladly so—
The song the Parcae once sang shuddering   1720
When Tantalus fell from his golden chair;
They suffered for their noble friend; grim were
Their hearts, and full of dread the song they sang.
Our nurse, when we were young, would sing it to
Us children, and I noted it with care.

     In fear of the gods let
     The race of man stand!
     Dominion they hold
     In hands everlasting,
     With power to use it   1730
     As they may see fit.

     One whom they exalt
     Should fear them twice over.
     On cliffs and on clouds
     Are chairs set out ready
     At tables of gold.

     If discord arises,
     The guests may be cast,
     Abused and dishonored,
     To the depths of the dark   1740
     And there wait in vain,
     Amid gloom and in fetters,
     For judgment with justice.

     Those others, however,

Sit endlessly feasting
At tables of gold.
And striding from mountain
Across unto mountain,
They scent from the chasms
The smoking breath   1750
Of the stifling Titans
Like a thin cloud of odor
Up-wafting from sacrifice.

These rulers avert
The eyes of their blessing
From whole generations,
Declining to see
In the grandson the grandsire's
Once well-beloved features
Now mute but eloquent.   1760

So sang the Parcae.
The old one, the exile,
He harkens in hollows
Of night to these songs,
Thinks children and grandchildren,
And shakes his head.   (1766)

ACT V

Thoas. Arkas.

ARKAS: Confused, I must admit I do not know
Which way I should turn my suspicion now.
Is it the captives who are secretly
Devising flight? Or can it be the priestess   1770
Who is assisting them? A growing rumor
Claims that the ship that brought those two men here
Is still concealed within some bay or other.
And that man's madness, and this consecration,
And all this holy pretext for delay
Call loudly for suspicion and precaution.
THOAS: Summon the priestess here immediately.
Then go and swiftly, sharply, search the coast
Down from the headland to the goddess' grove.
Forbear to probe its sacred depths, but lay   1780
A prudent ambush, fall upon them, seize
Them where you find them, as your custom is.
                  [*Exit Arkas.*]
Rage wildly alternates within my bosom,
First toward her whom I had held so holy,
Then toward myself, who by indulgence and
By kindness made her apt for treachery.
A human being soon adjusts to slavery
And soon learns to obey, if freedom is
Completely taken from him. Had she fallen
Into the hands of my rough ancestors,   1790
And if the holy savagery had spared her,
She would have been content to save herself

73

Alone, she would have gratefully accepted
Her fate, and would have termed it duty to
Shed alien blood before the altar
As need required. But as it is,
My kindness rouses rash desires in her.
In vain I hoped to join her fate to mine;
She now schemes for a private destiny.
By flattery she won my heart, and now   1800
That I resist that, she is seeking her
Own way by cunning and deceit, and all
My kindness seems to her a right of old.

[*Enter Iphigenia.*]

IPHIGENIA: You sent for me? What brings you to us here?
THOAS: You have delayed the sacrifice; why so?
IPHIGENIA: I have explained all that to Arkas, clearly.
THOAS: I wish to hear from you in more detail.
IPHIGENIA: The goddess grants you respite for reflection.
THOAS: This respite seems most opportune for *you.*
IPHIGENIA: If your heart has been steeled for this barbaric   1810
Decision, you should not have come! A king
Who asks inhuman actions will find henchmen
Enough who for reward and favor will
With greed accept half of the action's curse;
But his own presence still remains unblemished.
He sits within his stormcloud plotting death
And lets his messengers descend with flaming
Destruction on the luckless mortal's head,
While he serenely moves off in his storm,   1820
An unscathed god across the heights of sky.
THOAS: The holy lips intone a savage song.
IPHIGENIA: No priestess I, just Agamemnon's daughter.
The unknown woman's word you reverenced,
Now you abruptly give the princess orders?
No! From my youth I learned how to obey,
My parents first, then a divinity,
And in obedience I always felt

My soul most gloriously free; submission,
However, to a man's uncouth commands
I never did learn, either there or here.   1830
THOAS: An ancient law, not I, gives you this order.
IPHIGENIA: We seize with eagerness upon a law
    That serves our passion as an instrument.
    It is another and more ancient law
    That bids me to resist you now, the law
    By which all aliens are sacred.
THOAS: These captives seem to be dear to your heart,
    For in your sympathy and agitation
    You have forgotten the first rule of prudence:
    Not to irritate the man in power.   1840
IPHIGENIA: Whether I speak or not, you still can know
    What is and always will be in my heart.
    Will memory of a kindred destiny
    Not open any closed-up heart to pity?
    How much more mine! In them I see myself.
    Before the altar I myself once trembled
    And early death once awesomely surrounded
    Me as I knelt; the knife was lifted up
    That was to pierce my living bosom through.
    My inmost being cringed in reeling horror,   1850
    My eyes grew dim, and—then I woke up safe.
    Are we not bound to pay in turn to other
    Unfortunates what the gods granted us?
    And knowing this, and me, you still would force me?
THOAS: Obey your office, not your human master.
IPHIGENIA: Do not seek to extenuate the harshness
    That takes advantage of a woman's weakness.
    I am as free-born as a man. And if
    The son of Agamemnon stood before you,
    And if you asked improper things of him,   1860
    He has a sword and has an arm to wield it
    In his defense of the rights of his heart.
    But I have only words, and it beseems

A noble man to value women's words.

THOAS: I value them above a brother's sword.

IPHIGENIA: The fate of weapons wavers back and forth,
And no wise warrior underrates his foe.
But Nature has not left the weak defenseless
Either, against insolence and harshness.
She gives them joy in stratagem and cunning   1870
So they may dodge, delay, and circumvent.
Indeed, the man of power deserves the use of these.

THOAS: Precaution shrewdly parries cunning wiles.

IPHIGENIA: And no pure soul will have recourse to them.

THOAS: Do not imprudently pass your own sentence.

IPHIGENIA: O if you could but see how my soul struggles
To drive courageously away at first
Attack an evil seeking to possess it!
Do I stand here defenseless, then, against you?
My fair request, that gracious suppliant's branch   1880
More mighty in a woman's hand than sword
Or weapon, you reject and thrust aside:
What else is left me to defend myself?
Shall I beseech the goddess for a marvel?
Is there no strength in my soul's inner depths?

THOAS: The fate of those two foreigners disturbs you
Excessively, it seems. Who are they, pray,
For whom your spirit is so greatly roused?

IPHIGENIA: They are—they seem—I think that they are Greeks.

THOAS: They are compatriots of yours? and doubtless   1890
Awakened in you fair hopes of return?

IPHIGENIA (after a silence) :
Do men alone, then, have the right to do
Unheard-of feats? Can only men clasp things
Impossible to their heroic bosoms?[1]
What is termed great? What lifts to awe the souls
Of minstrels as they tell their oft-told tales,
Except what bravest men began with chances
Unlikely of success? He who by night

Stole up alone upon the enemy,
Then as an unexpected flame seized on   1900
The sleepers and raged in among the wakers
And finally, as hard-pressed by the wakened
He fled on foemen's horses, but with booty,—[2]
Shall he alone be praised? Or he alone
Who, spurning roads of safety, boldly went
A-roaming through the mountains and the forests
To clear the highwaymen out of a district?[3]
Is nothing left for us? Must gentle woman
Renounce her innate right, turn wild and fight
Against wild men, and wrest from you the right   1910
Of swords like Amazons who take revenge
In blood for their oppression? Back and forth
In my heart ebbs a daring enterprise;
I cannot help but meet with great reproach,
And even with dire harm, if I should fail;
Yet on your knees, ye gods, I lay it, and
If you are true, as you are said to be,
Then show it by your help and glorify
Truth through me!—Yes, I confess, O king,
A secret fraud is being perpetrated.   1920
You will in vain ask for those prisoners;
For they have gone—gone searching for their friends
Who with their ship are waiting by the shore.
The elder one, who was afflicted here
But who has now been cured—he is Orestes,
My brother, and the other one is his
Devoted friend since childhood, Pylades
By name. Apollo sends them here from Delphi
With his divine command to carry off
Diana's statue and to bring his sister   1930
Back to him there, in recompense for which
He promises deliverance to the man
Stained with his mother's blood and hounded by
The Furies. To your hands I thus entrust

Both remnants of the house of Tantalus.
Destroy us—if you *can*.
THOAS: You think the rough
And barbarous Scythian will hear the voice
Of truth and human decency that Atreus
The Greek would not hear?
IPHIGENIA: All men hear it, born
Beneath whatever sky they may, and through
Whose bosoms flows the fountainhead of life[4]   1940
Pure and unhindered.—What are you devising,
O king, in silence deep within your soul?
If it is our destruction, kill me first!
For now that there is no deliverance left
For us, I realize the ghastly peril
Into which I over-hastily
And wilfully have plunged my loved ones. Ah!
They will stand bound before me. With what looks
Can I take farewell of my brother then,   1950
Whose murderess I am? O, I can never
Again look into his beloved eyes!
THOAS: How the deceivers with their artful falsehoods
Have cast their nets about the head of one
Long cloistered and who readily lent ear
To their desires!
IPHIGENIA: No, no, O king! I could
Have been deceived, but these are loyal men
And true. And if you find them otherwise,
Then leave them to their fate and send me off
To exile as a punishment for folly   1960
Upon the bleak shore of some craggy island.
But if this man is my so long-besought
And much-loved brother, then release us; be
Kind to the brother as well as the sister.
My father died because of his wife's guilt,
And she died from her son. The final hope
Of Atreus' line now rests with him alone.

Let me with pure heart and pure hand go over
The sea and purify our family.
You will stand by your word!—If to my people   1970
Return were ever possible, you swore
To let me go. It now is possible.
A king will not, like vulgar men, consent
Out of embarrassment just to be rid
One moment of the suppliant; nor will
He promise for contingencies he hopes
Will not arise. He feels his full worth only
When he can gladden those who wait in hope.
THOAS: Impatiently, as fire contends with water
And, hissing, seeks extermination of   1980
Its enemy, so does the anger in
My bosom show resistance to your words.
IPHIGENIA: O let your mercy, circled round about
  With joy and praises and thanksgiving shine
Upon me like the steady altar-flame.
THOAS: How often has this strain brought me to calm!
IPHIGENIA: O, offer me your hand in sign of peace.
THOAS: You ask a great deal in so short a time.
IPHIGENIA: To do good things does not require reflection.
THOAS: It does! for sometimes out of good comes evil.   1990
IPHIGENIA: O, it is doubt that turns good into evil.
  Do not reflect; grant as your feelings prompt you.

                (*Enter Orestes under arms.*)

ORESTES (*speaking into the wings*):
  Redouble your best efforts! Hold them back!
  For these few moments only! Do not give
  Way to the mob, protect my and my sister's
  Way to the ship.

                (*to Iphigenia, without seeing the king*)
                Come! We have been betrayed.
  We have but small space left for flight. O hurry!

                (*He catches sight of the king.*)

THOAS (*putting his hand to his sword*):
Before me no man with impunity
Shall wield a naked sword.
IPHIGENIA: Do not profane
The goddess' dwelling place with rage and murder!   2000
Command your people to lay down their weapons,
And hear your priestess, hear your sister.
ORESTES: Tell me,
Who is this man who threatens us?
IPHIGENIA: Revere
In him the king who is my second father.
Forgive me, brother, but my childlike heart
Has placed our entire fate within his hand.
I have confessed the plan of you two men
And thereby saved my soul from treachery.
ORESTES: Then will he peaceably grant our return?
IPHIGENIA: Your flashing sword forbids my answering that.   2010
ORESTES (*putting up his sword*):
Speak, then. You see that I obey your word.

*(Enter Pylades, and soon after him
Arkas, both with drawn swords.)*

PYLADES: Do not delay! Our men are summoning
Their final strength. By giving ground they will
Be driven slowly back down to the sea.
But what discourse of princes do I find here!
This is the monarch's reverend head I see!
ARKAS: With calmness, as befits you well, O king,
You stand here and confront your enemies,
This insolence shall instantly be punished.
Their men retreat and die, their ship is ours;   2020
One word from you and it will be in flames.
THOAS: Go and proclaim a truce. No man of mine
Shall harm the foe so long as we are speaking.

(Exit Arkas.)

ORESTES: I will accept this truce. Dear friend, assemble

What men of ours are left and wait in patience
To see what end the gods assign our doings.
(*Exit Pylades.*)
IPHIGENIA: Deliver me from care before I start
To speak. I fear harsh quarrel if, O king,
You do not lend ear to the gentle voice
Of reasonableness, or you, my brother,   2030
Do not control the rashness of your youth.
THOAS: I shall restrain my anger, as beseems
The elder. Answer me. By what do you
Attest that you are Agamemnon's son,
This woman's brother here?
ORESTES: Here is the sword
With which he slew the doughty men of Troy.
I took it from his murderer and begged
The heaven-dwellers to bestow on me
The great king's arm and courage and good fortune
And to grant me a better death than his.   2040
Select one of the nobles from your army,
Confront me with the best one of them all.
As far as earth sustains the sons of heroes,
No alien is refused such a request.
THOAS: By ancient custom here such privilege
Was never granted strangers.
ORESTES: Then begin
A different custom with yourself and me!
In following it whole nations will translate
Their rulers' action into sacred law.
And let me not fight solely for our freedom,   2050
But let me, as an alien, fight for aliens.
If *I* die, then their sentence will have been
Pronounced along with mine; but if good fortune
Allows me to prevail, let no man ever
Set foot upon this shore without his being
Met by the swift glance of a helpful love,
And let all men depart therefrom consoled!

THOAS: You seem to be, youth, not unworthy of
  The line of ancestors in whom you glory.
  The count is large of brave and noble men   2060
  Who here attend me, but I still can face
  The foe myself at my age, and I am
  Prepared to try the chance of arms with you.
IPHIGENIA: By no means! For such bloody testimony
  There is, O king, no call! Withdraw hands from
  Your swords, and think of me and of my fate.
  A quick fight may immortalize a man,
  And even if he falls, the songs will praise him.
  But the unending tears thereafter shed
  By the surviving and deserted woman   2070
  No future age will count, and poets speak
  No word about the thousand days and nights
  Of weeping when a silent soul consumes
  Itself in vain with yearning to bring back
  The lost and suddenly departed friend.[5]
  An apprehension warned me at the outset
  Lest deception of some pirate might
  Abduct me from a place of safety and
  Traduce me into bondage. Diligently
  I questioned them, I probed each circumstance,   2080
  I asked for signs, and now my heart is certain.
  See here on his right hand the birthmark which
  Resembles, as it were, three stars, and which
  Appeared the very day that he was born.
  The priest said that it meant a grievous deed
  To be done by that hand. Then I am further
  Convinced twice over by this scar that furrows
  His eyebrow here. Once, when he was a child,
  Electra, quick and heedless as her manner
  Always was, dropped him out of her arms.   2090
  He struck against a tripod—[6] It is he—
  Must I speak too of his resemblance to
  His father, and the exultation of

My heart, as further proofs of my conviction?
THOAS: Even if your words resolved all doubts
And I restrained the anger in my heart,
Recourse to arms would still be needed to
Decide between us. I can see no peace.
They came here, as you have yourself acknowledged,
To steal my sacred statue of the goddess.   2100
Do you think I will calmly let them do so?
The Greeks have often turned their greedy eyes
On far-off treasures of barbarians—
The golden fleece, fine horses, lovely daughters;[7]
Not always did their force and guile, however,
Get them home safely with their stock of plunder.
ORESTES: The statue shall, O king, not cause us discord.
We now perceive the error which a god
Cast like a veil about our heads when he
Bade us set out upon our journey here.   2110
I had begged him for counsel and deliverance
From the Furies' company; he answered:
"If you will bring to Greece the sister who
On Tauris' shore now tarries in the temple
Against her will, the curse will be removed."
This we construed to mean Apollo's sister,
While he had *you* in mind! Your harsh bonds are
Now stricken off, and you, O holy one,
Are now restored to your own people. I
Have been healed at your touch; in your embrace   2120
The evil seized upon me with its claws
For the last time, and horribly it shook
Me to the very marrow; then it fled
Off like a serpent to its lair. Through you
I now enjoy the day's broad light once more.
Magnificent and fair now seems to me
The goddess' counsel. Like a sacred statue
Into which a city's fate is charmed
Unalterably by mystic words of gods,[8]

She took you, the protectress of the house,   2130
Away and kept you in a holy stillness
Unto your brother's and your people's blessing.
Then when all rescue on the wide earth seemed
To have been lost, you give us back all things
Again. Allow your soul to turn to peace,
O king! Do not prevent her from completing
The consecration of her father's house,
From giving me back to my now pure hall
And placing on my head my ancient crown.
Requite the blessing that she brought to you   2140
By letting me enjoy my closer right.
Men's highest glory, violence and cunning,
Are by the truth of this exalted soul
Now put to shame, and pure and childlike trust
In a high-minded man meets with reward.

IPHIGENIA: Remember your sworn word and let yourself
Be swayed by this speech from an upright man's
True lips. O look at us! It is not often
You have occasion for such noble action.
You cannot well refuse it; grant it soon!   2150

THOAS: Then go!

IPHIGENIA: Not thus, my king! Without your blessing,
With your ill-will, I shall not part from you.
O do not banish us. A friendly guest-right
Must be the rule between us: that way we
Are not cut off forever. For you are
As dear to me as ever was my father,
And this impression is fixed in my soul.
And if the least among your people ever
Brings to my ear the cadence of the voice
I am so used to hear from you, or if   2160
I see the poorest man dressed in your manner,
I shall receive him like a god, I shall
Myself prepare a couch for him, myself
Invite him to a seat beside the fire,

Inquiring news of you and of your fate.
O may the gods give you well-merited
Reward for your good deeds and for your kindness!
Farewell. O turn your face toward us and give
Me back a gracious word of parting now!
For then the wind will swell the sails more gently   2170
And tears more soothingly flow from the eyes
Of those who part. Farewell, and as a pledge
Of ancient friendship give me your right hand.
THOAS: Farewell!   (2174)

NOTES

1. The crime of Tantalus the Titan was variously identified in antiquity:

(a) he stole ambrosia and nectar (immortality-bestowing food and drink of the gods) and gave them to mankind;

(b) he served his own son as food for the gods, to test their omniscience;

(c) he betrayed the secrets of the gods;

(d) he boasted in overweening pride (*hybris*) of his association with the gods.

Goethe disregards the first two of these, vaguely alludes to the third, and stresses the fourth.

For his crime Tantalus was condemned to Tartarus,—which Homer describes as a pit as far below Hades as earth is below heaven,—there to stand up to his chin in water beneath a loaded fruit-tree, both water and fruit forever receding as he sought to satisfy his thirst and hunger.

2. Pelops competed with Oenomaüs in a chariot race for the hand of Hippodamia. With the promise of half of his future kingdom, if he won, Pelops bribed Myrtilus, his opponent's charioteer, to loosen the linch-pins in his opponent's chariot-wheels, with the result that Oenomaüs was killed in the race. Instead of keeping his promise to Myrtilus once he had become king, Pelops had the charioteer thrown into the sea. The drowning man cursed his murderer and all of Pelops' descendants.

3. Chrysippus was Pelops' first son, by the nymph Axioche. See the genealogical chart at the end of the Introduction to this play.

4. The motif of Hippodamia's suicide, like other details of Iphigenia's narrative, derive from the *Fabulae* of C. Ilius Hyginus.

5. Euripides, Hyginus, and Ovid (*Metamorphoses* xii, 27) tell of Iphigenia's rescue from death at the sacrificial altar; Sophocles (in *Electra*) and Æschylus (in *Agamemnon*) say she died there at Aulis.

ACT II

1. The Furies, who haunt murderers. They come from the ghost realms of the underworld, and hence are "Subterraneans," (line 581).

2. Pylades was outlawed as an accomplice in Clytemnestra's murder.

3. Goethe here follows Euripides' *Electra,* where it is related that an old servant stole the lad Orestes away and took him to Strophius, King of Phocis, who had married Agamemnon's sister Anaxibia; Pylades, the son of Strophius, was therefore Orestes' cousin. See the genealogical chart at the end of the Introduction and also lines 1009-1014 of Act III.

4. To the Greeks almost any nomad north and east of the Black Sea was a "Scythian."

ACT III

1. The lake, nine miles west of Italian Naples, which was, according to Italian lore, the entrance to the underworld.

2. Again Goethe tells the story as Sophocles told it in *Electra.*

3. A river of the underworld.

4. The Furies were forced off the earth and into the underworld by the gods at the same time when the gods defeated and imprisoned the Titans.

5. The Gorgon Medusa's head turned beholders to stone.

6. The bridal raiment which jealous Medea sent to her rival Creusa burst into flames and consumed the bride.—Hercules died of a poisoned shirt.

7. Lyaeus—Bacchus.

8. Tantalus.

9. Both Apollo and his sister Artemis could shoot unseen arrows of death against mortals.

10. The Eumenides, literally "the gracious ones," is the euphemistic name for the Furies.

ACT IV

1. The island of Delos.

2. The (Roman) gods of the hearth, known as the Lares and Penates.

3. Old reliefs represent the Titans as having vulture claws.

ACT V

1. Perhaps as Hercules clasped and strangled the Nemean lion.

2. Like Ulysses or Diomedes who in Book X on the *Iliad* raided the camp of the Thracians to prevent the latter from helping the Trojans.

3. Like Theseus in dealing with Sciros, Procrustes, etc.

4. The "fountainhead of life" = *fons vitae*, a periphrasis for "God."

5. Laodamia's tears moved the gods to return her husband Protesilaus to her from beyond death for three hours' time. (See Wordsworth's poem, *Laodamia*.)

6. Euripides' *Electra* mentions such a scar, acquired while chasing a fawn.

7. The golden fleece was stolen from the land of Colchis by Jason.—Hercules took the magical horses of Laomedon when he captured Troy.—Beautiful daughters, e.g. Ariadne of Crete, Helen of Sparta, Medea of Colchis.

8. Such a statue was the palladium, or sacred image of Athene, which fell from the skies and which preserved Troy until it was stolen by Ulysses and Diomedes.